Heaven in Ordinary

Heaven in Ordinary

Poetry and Religion in a Secular Age

David Jasper

The Lutterworth Press

The Lutterworth Press
P.O. Box 60
Cambridge
CB1 2NT
United Kingdom

www.lutterworth.com
publishing@lutterworth.com

ISBN: 978 0 7188 9541 9

British Library Cataloguing in Publication Data
A record is available from the British Library

First published by The Lutterworth Press, 2018

We are thankful to Bloodaxe Books for the permission
to include in this book David Scott's quotations, and to
Oxford University Press for the permission to include
Sir Geoffrey Hill's quotations.

For Hannah, Ruth and May

Contents

1.
Introduction

This little book has its origins in the St Aidan's Lectures, given at the invitation of Dr Nicholas Taylor in May 2018 in St Aidan's Episcopal Church, Clarkston near Glasgow, of which he is the Rector. These lectures are an established annual event in the city, an opportunity for members of the congregation, local people, visitors from the universities, schools and other churches in Glasgow to listen to talks on a variety of subjects within the life of the church that demand a kind of leisurely but acute form of attention to matters of cultural importance. Such attention is all too rare in the life of today's harassed, numerically declining and often self-absorbed church in our society. I thank Nicholas for his kind invitation and for granting me an opportunity that has, on my part, an undeniable degree of self-indulgence, but offers me an opportunity to reflect upon almost a lifetime – I can set it precisely at a period of fifty two years since I was fourteen years old when I fell in love with poetry (a story to be told shortly) – during which time the relationship between poetry and religion has been with me as an ever-abiding concern, stimulus and puzzle to the heart, mind and spirit.

Any writing, and perhaps the more so as one grows older, has an ineradicable autobiographical element in it, sometimes more obvious, sometimes less, and this book is no exception. The predominantly

Anglican nature of my taste in poetry will be quickly evident, not surprisingly since my father was an Anglican priest. I have been ordained and served in the Church of England and the Scottish Episcopal Church for more than forty years, and, incidentally, have a retired Anglican bishop as a brother-in-law. Anglicanism is, one might say, in my blood, heart and mind, and however critical I might be of the Anglican Communion, however perilously close I have been at times to jumping ship, I am still on board and will probably remain so until the end. One cannot but be aware of the failings of those institutions which one loves most dearly. But if I am also grateful to the University of Oxford for initiating me into whatever understanding of Christian theology I now possess, I am far more indebted to my earlier experience of reading English literature at Jesus College, Cambridge where I was taught by, among others, Raymond Williams, a man of great humanity and wisdom and no Christian belief. Behind him, I am indebted to a remarkable teacher of English at school, the late Laurie Jagger, who first opened my eyes to the poetry of Thomas Hardy, and after that Shakespeare, Milton and a miscellaneous group of twentieth century poets from W.B. Yeats to Stephen Spender, Philip Larkin and, rather unwillingly on my part, I have to admit, T.S. Eliot. Laurie, I know, influenced the lives of many people, some far more distinguished in the field of literature and the arts than I, in profound and often hidden ways. He could not go unmentioned in this book, over which his benign spirit rests in so many ways.

Thomas Hardy's poetry was my first love in English literature, and Hardy will have a whole chapter to himself very early in this book. My selection of five poets, not in any particular chronological order, will seem odd and arbitrary to most people, but they make perfectly good sense to me: Thomas Hardy, Samuel Taylor Coleridge, Thomas Traherne, Sir Philip Sidney and Sir Geoffrey Hill. Finally, I will give some attention to the poets of the English pastoral tradition from Chaucer to R.S. Thomas and beyond. I make no apology for the a-historical order of the chapters. They reflect the history of my own poetic encounters with English poetry and religion, and the order makes sense to me.

Together, these poets reflect a variety of attitudes towards Anglicanism, both for and against, that sum up, to a degree, my own complex relationship with that tradition within the Christian church. Not accidentally these chapters conclude with poets, most of them priests, within the enduring pastoral tradition that is, and must be, at the very heart of Anglicanism in its different forms. But it is Thomas Hardy who comes first, a writer described recently as 'the churchiest skeptic'[1] – an individual who can never quite get away from the practice of a religious tradition, whose theological roots he had lost somewhere in the darkness of his gloomy soul, perhaps not surprisingly given the institutional rigidity of so much Victorian Anglicanism. But Hardy goes on, hoping it might be so and never entirely losing sight of the vision glorious. And it was Hardy who took me back a step in time to S.T. Coleridge, to whose thought and poetry I devoted my doctoral studies in Durham under the careful eye of Ann Loades. Coleridge was, perhaps with John Henry Newman, the greatest English Christian thinker of the nineteenth century, a troubled soul with moments of extraordinary poetic vision. Coleridge can be infuriating, but he was, finally, an honest man, and that is worth a great deal in our world.

In the seventeenth century, Thomas Traherne stands in complete contrast to these troubled nineteenth century souls. Much of his writings in both prose and verse have only recently been discovered and edited, and are still in the process of publication in a magnificent projected nine volume *Complete Works* edited by Jan Ross,[2] though you do not need to read very much of his poetry or prose to sense the essence of Traherne. He was one of those rare people who carry profound learning lightly, and he had an extraordinary capacity to see the unity of all created things under God. If Hardy's late Victorian world is beginning to fall apart, Traherne, two centuries earlier, sees everything together as a whole, as Coleridge had also struggled to do in his aesthetic sense of 'unity in multeity' that is nothing less than 'the language of God himself, as uttered by Nature'.[3] At the beginning of his unfinished *Commentaries of Heaven*, identified as his writing as late as 1981, Traherne proposes that:

---

1. John Fawell, Hardy: 'The Churchiest Skeptic', ed. by Ineke Bocktin, Jennifer Kilgore-Caradec and Cathy Parc, *Poetry and Religion: Figures of the Sacred* (Bern: Peter Lang, 2013), pp. 169-180.
2. *The Works of Thomas Traherne.* ed. by Jan Ross. 9 Volumes (Cambridge: Brewer 2005-). The work is projected to be completed by 2020.
3. S.T. Coleridge, *Hints Towards the Formation of a More Comprehensive Theory of Life* (London: John Churchill, 1848] Facsimile (Farnborough: Gregg International, 1970), pp. 42, 17.

The Mysteries of Felicitie
are opened
and
ALL THINGS
Discovered
to be
Objects of Happiness.[4]

After Traherne we go back in time even further to the English
Renaissance and to Sir Philip Sidney. In the very best sense of the term
Sidney was a Christian gentleman. That latter title is perhaps not very
fashionable these days, but it remains important that a poet and a
Renaissance man, a translator of the Psalms and writer of love sonnets
in the Petrarchan tradition should represent for us that necessary figure
of the 'gentle – man'. The same quality of gentleness, perhaps, cannot be
so easily said of my last individual poet and the most recent, Sir Geoffrey
Hill. I never met Hill, but I somehow feel that I know him through the
saintly medium of Peter Walker, Bishop of Ely, to whom I owe so much,
and it was Peter who introduced me to the difficult treasures of Hill's
profoundly religious verse. Hill's poems written between 1952 and 2012
are also now available in one large, splendid volume edited by Kenneth
Haynes.[5]

Finally, I cannot omit the chapter on the tradition of English pastoral
poetry that has its beginnings in Geoffrey Chaucer's 'Poor Parson of
the Town', and remains flourishing in a quiet way today. For this we
should be thankful. It is attractive to me for its quality of hiddenness,
even its uselessness in worldly terms, an ecclesial virtue that we are
sometimes in danger of losing in the Anglican tradition as it now suffers
the seductions of missionary ambition and the zeal of bureaucratic
efficiency. The way of love is quieter, less anxious, perhaps.

But I do not want this to be just another book on Christianity and
English poetry. In one of my earliest books on the relationship between
literature and theology, I wrote a chapter on the complex critical
tradition in English that relates poetry to religion, from Sidney, through
Dr Samuel Johnson in the eighteenth century, up to Lord David Cecil,
the editor of the first *Oxford Book of Christian Verse*, T.S. Eliot and
more recent critics like my former colleague in Durham, the late Ruth

---

4   *The Works of Thomas Traherne*, Volume 2 (Cambridge: Brewer, 2007), p. 1.
5.   Geoffrey Hill, *Broken Hierarchies: Poems 1952-2012*, ed. by Kenneth Haynes,
      (Oxford: Oxford University Press, 2013).

Etchells.[6] I will come back to that reflection in my 'Conclusion' to this book. The relationship between poetry and religion is never easy, ranging from Samuel Johnson's complete separation of poetry from the matter of religion – a view descended from such anxieties as Andrew Marvell's fear that Milton's biblical *Paradise Lost* would bring about the 'ruin of sacred truths'[7] – to, on the other hand, the complete merger of poetry with the stuff of religion, prayer and perhaps even theology. The reflections on five English poets in the present book are not in any way supposed to be 'prayerful' or even particularly religious. My position is very different from that of Ruth Etchells who once wrote in a little book entitled *Praying with the English Poets* (1990):

> the mystery of prayer has this in common with the mystery of poetry, that their language ranges from the commonplace and the (literally) mundane, to fervency, exaltation, and rapt stillness. Noisy as gongs, quiet as breath, musical, abrasive, an undertone, a declamation.[8]

It is not that there is no truth in this, of the kind to be found when we are reading the poetry of George Herbert, and certainly Thomas Traherne or Henry Vaughan. (It is something oddly more difficult to find outside the seventeenth century.) But underlying the present book is a very much more difficult and indeed challenging sense of this complex relationship between poetry and religion.

The reason that I have worried about these connections between theology (and religion) and literature for most of my life is because I think that their relationship is absolutely necessary, but at the same time highly problematic and even obscure. First of all, there is great danger in simply confusing the two, as many people tend to do. Poets may or may not be particularly 'religious', but often the most 'religious' of them might be writing in deep rebellion against, or in an understandable rejection of, such things as churches or other institutions of religion, their beliefs and demands. Hardy was like that. Others, like Traherne, are the complete opposite of this in their sense of poetry and divinity. As regards theology, poetry is certainly more

---

6   David Jasper, *The Study of Literature and Religion: An Introduction*, 2nd edn, (London: Macmillan, 1992), pp. 10-14.

7   Andrew Marvell, 'On Mr. Milton's Paradise Lost', *The Poems*, ed. by Hugh MacDonald (London: Routledge and Kegan Paul, 1952), p. 64.

8   Ruth Etchells, *Praying with the English Poets* (London: SPCK, 1990), pp. vii-viii.

fundamental and anterior to all possible theological articulation. One way of describing it is to construe poetry as a prolegomenon to religion and theology. It is a field or space into which religion might be called as appropriate, though often in strange and, to itself, unaccustomed ways. What I am talking about is something like the French thinker Maurice Blanchot's idea of *l'espace littéraire*, and there are few thinkers more important for the beginning of the study of literature and theology than Blanchot. It was he, after all, who recognised that the tragedy of Kafka was that he was an inveterate man of literature who had a finally hopeless preoccupation with the religious demand of salvation. Kafka's passion is literary, wrote Blanchot, but salvation is an enormous preoccupation with him, all the stronger because it is hopeless, and all the more hopeless because it is totally uncompromising.[9] I think that I can understand that and it explains to me at least why reading Kafka is both so painful and so necessary. Of this *espace littéraire*, Blanchot wrote:

> A book . . . has a centre which attracts it. This centre is not fixed, but it is displaced by the pressure of the book and circumstances of its composition. Yet it is also a fixed centre which, if it is genuine, displaces itself, while remaining the same and becoming always more central, more hidden, more uncertain and more imperious.[10]

It is this tension between the unfixed and hidden centre, shifted by the pressure of writing, and that centre which is necessarily fixed with its imperious demands, that is so important. In this tension, literature, and above all poetry, far from being a 'handmaid of piety' (as John Wesley once called it in his 1780 Preface to *Hymns for the People Called Methodists*) is the very opposite, but yet the site within which religion and theology are endlessly questioned and reformed.

I mentioned at the beginning that I was fortunate enough to be a student at Cambridge when Raymond Williams, at the height of his fame as an intellectual figure in the New Left, was teaching there in the late '60s and early '70s. One of his most prominent students at Jesus College, a little ahead of me in time, was Terry Eagleton, and Terry's recent work *Culture and the Death of God* (2014) was very much a formative influence

---

9   Maurice Blanchot, *The Space of Literature*, trans. by Ann Smock (Lincoln, Nebraska: University of Nebraska Press, 1982), p. 57.

10   Frontispiece to *The Space of Literature*.

upon this present book and the Glasgow lectures that lie behind as they were being brought to birth. Eagleton reminds us that since the European Enlightenment, and in our own European age of drastically shrinking churches and widespread public neglect of traditional faith, religion is actually extremely difficult to eradicate or even ignore. Thomas Hardy, of course, knew that long ago, and that is another reason why I begin with him. On the first page of his book Eagleton writes:

> I start by showing how God survived the rationalism of the eighteenth century, and conclude with his dramatic reappearance in our own supposedly faithless age.[11]

Furthermore, it is as well to keep reminding ourselves that religion is by no means necessarily a good thing. If genuine atheists are more often than not rather reluctant atheists, fundamentalists of any kind – Christian, Islamic or whatever – are the inevitable products of a cultural situation that has suffered for some time from a toxic disingenuousness. Western liberalism since the eighteenth century, both in religious and political terms, has actually only got itself largely to blame for the rigid, dogmatic and unlovely violence of the fundamentalist and the equally unlovely amorality of our present so-called political 'populism'. Truth is never an easy concept, and religion in its many guises in western societies in these last few hundred years has had an uphill task. Its demise as a liberal enterprise cannot be a matter for much surprise. To start with, it has been overburdened (or overburdened itself) with its task as our moral gatekeeper, a responsibility that should begin much closer to home simply in our sense of being human. Eagleton puts it this way:

> If religious faith were to be released from the burden of furnishing social orders with a set of rationales for their existence, it might be free to rediscover its true purpose as a critique of all such politics.[12]

---

11 Terry Eagleton, *Culture and the Death of God* (New Haven and London: Yale University Press, 2015), p. viii.

12 Ibid. p. 207. It was a point made in a rather different tone by Richard Holloway, the former Bishop of Edinburgh, in his very readable book *Godless Morality: Keeping Religion out of Ethics* (Edinburgh: Canongate, 1999). I applaud heartily the paradox that drives Richard's argument, that 'our attempt to love morally as though there were no God might be the final test of faith'. It might, indeed, 'Be God's greatest triumph'. (p. 5.) Here we must delve our deepest humanity – and poetry is often very good at that.

That is very true, and as a clergyman, I am sick to death of being asked to state a *position* – on firm theological grounds – in matters of gender, the ending of life, and so on. We somehow feel sure that theology (and behind it, in some mysterious, unintelligible way, the Bible) will come up with the final answer, embalmed in history and tradition. More often than not it won't and it shouldn't. Such theological entrancements are generally simply ways of maintaining the *status quo* and they have a nasty tendency to distance us from our proper humanity. As Eagleton puts it in another, earlier book, *After Theory*, the Yahweh of the opening chapters of the Book of Isaiah thunders his exasperation at his 'pathologically cultic people' retorting that instead 'he will be known for what he is . . . when they see the stranger being made welcome, the hungry being filled with good things, and the rich being sent empty away.'[13] When we learn to become properly human then we shall begin to know something of God.

I end my brief encounter with Eagleton's work with his own closing words in *Culture and the Death of God* on the impropriety of calling in 'supernatural support' for 'common-or-garden morality', and regarding:

> The grossly inconvenient news that our forms of life must undergo radical dissolution if they are to be reborn as just and compassionate communities. The sign of that dissolution is a solidarity with the poor and the powerless. It is here that a new configuration of faith, culture and politics might be born.[14]

It is not just that religion won't go away – and if we think it has then it usually reappears all too often in very nasty forms. Religion is something that needs to be continually altered and reflected upon in endlessly changing and profoundly human cultural circumstances. It begins in our humanity in all its frailty and not in any bold statements about God. Look at the beginning of Psalm 22 (which Jesus speaks from on the cross[15]) or Psalm 130 – *De Profundis*, a cry from the abyss. The point is that in these deeply 'religious' moments God is *not* there, and so I am not here saying anything much about God, at least to start with. I happen to think (and have always thought) that

---

13 Terry Eagleton, *After Theory* (London: Allen Lane, 2003), p. 175.

14 *Culture and the Death of God*, p. 208.

15 Mark 15: 34, Matthew 27: 46.

Nietzsche, in his wildly and often extravagantly 'poetic' way, got it just about right in *The Gay Science* (1863) in his parable about the death of one particular god – though it depends, of course, very much upon what you think you mean by the idea of God. There's the rub, and I will leave it there for the moment. In due course the poetry can speak for itself.[16]

In my experience, theologians and others who subscribe in some sense to the idea of the death of God are almost always the most deeply God-haunted people. It is very often in the words and writings of poets, whether believers or not, that such hauntings are most profoundly and disturbingly expressed. Here, I suppose, we are at the very heart of this book. The poet is a person of ambivalence. In 1798, Samuel Taylor Coleridge in 'Kubla Khan' famously warns us to fear the poet with his flashing eyes and floating hair:

> Weave a circle round him thrice,
> And close your eyes with holy dread,
> For he on honey-dew hath fed,
> And drunk the milk of Paradise.[17]

The poet is to be feared, but it is because the poet alone has returned to the Paradise Garden from which we have been banished, and that is, after all, just a dream. The poet is also to be loved. Here we are at the meeting point of the sacred and the profane in the mystery of words. Anyone – and it is most of us at some point or other – who has felt both the seductive pull and the dislike of 'religion' at some time or another, will find in the poet the splendours and the miseries of the religious life with or without God, and its endless, necessary and glorious fascinations.

As I have said, the choice of these five poets in this book is entirely personal. There could have been easier and perhaps more straightforward choices, made from, perhaps, George Herbert to W.B. Yeats. The poetry that you like and resonate with, rather after the manner of people, is to some extent accidental and personal. I can

---

16 I have long felt myself drawn close to Tom Altizer's sense of the radical Christian, the Christian 'who believe[s] that the Church and Christendom have sealed Jesus in his tomb.' Thomas J. J. Altizer and William Hamilton, *Radical Theology and the Death of God* (Harmondsworth: Penguin, 1968), p. 182.

17 Samuel Taylor Coleridge, *Poetical Works*, ed. by Ernest Hartley Coleridge (Oxford: Oxford University Press, 1969), p. 298.

well imagine that Philip Sidney is not to everyone's taste these days – he does seem to us rather formal, remote, and a bit stand-offish. But he speaks to me and I have known him for a very long time. And you do not choose whom you fall in love with. You just know it when it happens. The demands of Christian theology and the canon of Scripture are quite strict and in some ways limited. The canon of poetry (as indeed of all literature) is far more expansive and much more broadly hospitable. It doesn't actually matter if you find you do not really like Sidney's poetry and his Psalms that take you back in a particular manner, as we shall see, to the poetry of the Bible. There are plenty of other poets ready to invite you to taste and see. But at least pause a while and let me introduce him to you, perhaps for the first time or perhaps as someone forgotten since school days. Listen to why he is important for me, and try to understand why, for me, reading the *Sidney Psalter* of Sir Philip and Mary Sidney is a way into something like 'religion' because here the Psalms are embraced by a certain English poetics. And, as with people (or music), you can grow to like some poetry that you find difficult at first.

Many years ago I read, more from a sense of duty than anything else, Harold Bloom's large book on *The Western Canon* (1994). It is certainly worth a read, like most of Bloom's writings, but there is a tone about it that is, I believe, profoundly wrong. It suffers from too much nostalgia, which is always very enervating, and tends towards a kind of intellectual and cultural élitism that is off-putting and ultimately deadly when you are trying to encourage people to read poetry and they begin by being rather afraid of it. I have tried to avoid both of these sins that particularly afflict academics and often also people of a 'religious persuasion', not least the clergy. I have always felt that the religious life is not something that is achieved, but something towards which, at best, we can say we are moving. If you want to use a religious term, then my encounters with poetry are, at best, most appropriately described as moments of salvation,[18] experiences of healing that bind up the wounds and keep us on the road. Poetry is the best thing for such healing, its salt cleansing even while it irritates, its balm also as smooth as olive oil when needed. Only through the poetic process does the stuff of religion begin to make real sense to me.

---

18 I am thinking here of Primo Levi's collection of stories from within Auschwitz, *Moments of Reprieve* (1981, English translation, 1986)

Very recently I reviewed a book of essays published posthumously. They were the writings of a former student of mine who achieved her doctorate in Glasgow University when she was a sprightly seventy-five years old. Kay Carmichael's *It Takes a Lifetime to Become Yourself* (2017) was edited from her papers and poems by her husband, David Donnison. Kay was damaged terribly in her childhood by the church and never got over that trauma. But she was a deeply religious person for all that – I mean a deeply committed person in every sense of the word, and at her most heart-felt moments she expressed herself in poetry. She was not a great poet, but that does not matter. We should all write poetry from time to time. One of the tributes for Kay's funeral described her as 'a naughty, dignified, compassionate rebel with a cause'.[19] It struck me at the time as a perfect description of the Jesus Christ whom I try to follow, though it might be better just to think of Kay as herself and not confuse her with impossible precedents that she certainly would not have liked very much. The book that emerged from her doctoral study was entitled *Sin and Forgiveness: New Responses in a Changing World* (2003). It was an enquiry into how sin (which is different from immorality) and forgiveness should be understood in a post-Christian society, grounded in Kay's assertion that the Christian paradigm of sin and forgiveness was generally too simplistic, too 'doctrinal' and too determined.

Like many teachers I have learnt far more from my students than I suspect they ever learnt from me. I go back continually to the poets from theology, because they know very well that life and all of its issues are far more complex, far more nuanced and often far less simplistic than anything theology can finally deal with. Of course we need rules, but all rules are there to be broken in the end, even if it means taking the punishment as a result.

There are plenty of excellent books on poetry and religion, dealing with the power of the imagination, the matter of spirituality, the question of symbol, and so on. Most of them, I admit, I find a bit dull and predictable, so I won't mention any names here, but you will find a few listed in the bibliography at the end of this book. These brief chapters are, I hope, a little different. They reflect a love affair with poetry where meaning and problems have their beginnings. Here 'religion' is paused

---

19 Kay Carmichael, *It Takes a Lifetime to Become Yourself*, ed. by David Donnison (Edinburgh: Scotland Street Press, 2017), p. 231. The words are of Anthony (Lord) Lester.

for a moment, though it is really what the whole thing is about. We start in the poet's world and in what W.B. Yeats called, in 'The Circus Animals' Desertion', that rag and bone shop of the heart where truth begins to appear in the beauty and the confusion - and then we go forward again, hoping it might be so.

Thomas Hardy
(1840-1928)

2

Thomas Hardy:
Faith and Doubt

This little book is, as I have suggested in the Introduction, a kind of an account of my love affair with poetry in its religious aspects that has extended over more than half a century since my days at school. Long before my mind turned to questions of theology or I felt the beginnings of a call to the ordained ministry, I fell in love with verse and its language, not only in English, but in Greek and Latin too, especially the poetry of Homer in Doric Greek and Virgil in his stately Latin. Such was an English public school education in those days. I have made that admission, so that is out of the way. And as with most love affairs, especially when we are very young, it is the first moment that stands clearest in the memory, the first kiss, as it were. For me it was reading Thomas Hardy's early poem 'Neutral Tones' at the age of thirteen and finding there the power of words in poetry to say the unsayable, beyond all reason, still making sense in a world that yet remains so often without sense; not logical or rational sense, but a kind of 'knowing'. It was actually Hardy's tragic voice that made the music of Shakespeare faintly audible to me for the first time – the last, unbearable scenes of *King Lear*, or those troubling words of the ageing, world-weary Prospero to his daughter Miranda in *The Tempest* about the brave new world that is hers, not his – ''tis new . . . to thee'. This chapter will stay almost entirely with Hardy – not only with his tragic voice, but with his boundless love of life, of dancing and pretty girls (a weakness, or perhaps a strength, that never left him, as was true also of Yeats), of nature and sweet cider, and his sense of the glory and bitterness of human love captured in his extraordinary *Poems of 1912-13*, written after the death of his first wife, Emma.[1]

In the coming pages we shall stay awhile with our five English poets, and then a further group of particularly 'religious' poets – not, as I have already said, in chronological order, but in the order that they came to me. The poet Philip Larkin once said that W.B. Yeats was the greatest of modern poets, but that Thomas Hardy was his favourite.[2] Hardy, for me too, must always come first. In subsequent chapters we shall turn back in time from the nineteenth century (after a look at Coleridge) to the seventeenth century and to the verse of Thomas Traherne, a far more Christian poet than Hardy (though perhaps not more religious), a gentle, scholarly visionary with mystical insight and a view of the world that sees God in all things and in all places. Then we will go back even further, to the sixteenth century and to the poetry and prose of Sir Philip Sidney – that Renaissance man *par excellence* – for whom poetry was a making of worlds, its golden visions alive in a world of fallen humanity, and who, with his sister Mary, Countess of Pembroke, gave us a version of the Psalms in glorious Elizabethan English, their music and rhythms tutored by the poetry of Petrarch and the Italian Renaissance. Sidney was not only English, he was deeply European and would have disdained the direction of our current national politics. Then, finally, in this tour of individual poets, we come back into our own time and that craggy, difficult, most anguished of English poets Sir Geoffrey Hill, one-time professor of literature and religion at Boston University, taking us back again to the languages of the unsayable and reminding us that words are living things,[3] that in the beginning was the Word, and that words, rightly said, can still salve and save our souls.

And what of theology? That is, at its simplest, the word of God – in Greek *theos* meaning God and *logos* meaning word. Theology, at its living, enacted heart, must begin with words and in poetry – that term

---

1   Published in Hardy's collection of poems *Satires of Circumstance* (1914).

2   Philip Larkin, Introduction to *The North Ship* (London: Faber and Faber, 1966), p. 10. Larkin chose more poems by Hardy (28) in his *Oxford Book of Twentieth Century English Verse* (1973) than by any other poet.

3   The phrase is from S.T. Coleridge, and I shall come back to it in more detail in the next chapter.

being taken from another Greek word *poiesis*, which literally means to make something out of nothing, like God in the beginning in an act of speaking that was, in Christian theology at least, a moment of (to switch from Greek to Latin) *creatio ex nihilo* – a creation out of nothing. God, then, we might say, is the greatest of all poets. Theology is not, in the beginning, so much *thought* but *felt* and known in words and in the space of literature that thrives on the intrigues of metaphor and metonymy, irony and synecdoche, paradox, understatement, and so on.

But now let us allow Hardy to take over. Few would dispute that one of his greatest poems, written in 1899, and published on 31 December 1900, is 'The Darkling Thrush'. It opens with these lines:

> I leant upon a coppice gate
>   When Frost was spectre-gray.
> And Winter's dregs made desolate
>   The weakening eye of day. [4]

Few at the same time acknowledged that behind its bleak portrait of the world lies John Keats' glorious 'Ode to a Nightingale'. These two birds – Hardy's aged thrush and Keats' immortal nightingale seem the very opposite of one another – that of Keats (though himself, 'darkling I listen') being the dark beauty of the summer night, 'not born for death, immortal Bird',[5] Hardy's thrush shivering in the depths of winter, 'an aged thrush, frail, gaunt, and small/In blast-beruffled plume'. The nightingale sings with 'full-throated ease', yet the thrush offers, in spite of its fragility and all the misery of the world, 'a full-hearted evensong/ of joy illimited'. Thomas Hardy is that most religious of beings, a man caught between belief and unbelief, something between an agnostic and an atheist, who attended the services of the Church of England to the end of his life, if only, perhaps, to please his wife, and a man who could be gripped by a profound pessimism. And yet, that fragile thrush sings, in mid-winter, an evensong that celebrates: 'Some blessed Hope, whereof he knew/And I was unaware.' It is typically Hardy. The poet writes of that of which he has no knowledge, a hope that exists only in the song of a bird that he himself has created *ex nihilo* in his poetry.

---

4   Thomas Hardy, *The Collected Poems* (London: Macmillan, 1965), p. 137. (Henceforth, *CP*).

5   John Keats, *Selected Poetry and Letters*, ed. by Richard Harter Fogle (San Francisco: Rinehart Press, 1969), p. 248.

Hardy never quite gives up. Best known as a novelist, he was, at heart, a poet, though his earliest published poems were hated by the critics; his first collection entitled *Wessex Poems* (1898) was dismissed as 'slovenly, slipshod, uncouth verses, stilted in sentiment, poorly conceived and worse wrought'.[6] His greatest novels, for which he was revered and eventually in the end castigated[7] – *The Mayor of Casterbridge* (1886), *The Woodlanders* (1887), *Tess of the D'Urbervilles* (1891), *Jude the Obscure* (1896) – all end on notes of tragedy or seeming despair, portraits of what Hardy described as 'the tragical conditions of life'. He was brought up a practising Christian and even briefly contemplated ordination, like many young men at some stage of their lives, and his loss of Christian belief and faith in the church never quite eradicated hope: not quite. He followed some of the fashionable alternatives to Christianity in his day – the rather dotty Positivism of Auguste Comte, for example, who preached a cheerful religion of humanity based on 'scientific' principles – even while at the same time he could not quite shed the profound pessimism of the German thinker Arthur Schopenhauer who saw the world as purely malicious and God merely an illusion. In 1922, at the end of Hardy's long life and after knowing the trauma of the First World War, he expressed a sense that humankind might yet be 'drawing back for a spring', adding:

> I forlornly hope so, notwithstanding the supercilious regard of hope by Schopenhauer, von Hartmann and other philosophers down to Einstein, who have my respect.[8]

He added that his faith in the church as the means 'to keep the shreds of morality together' was dim:

> [O]ne must not be sanguine in reading signs . . . that the Church will go far in the removal of "things that are shaken" has not been encouraging.[9]

Some things, it might be said, never change.

---

6   Unsigned review in *Saturday Review*, 7 January 1899, lxxxvii, 19. (Reprinted in R.G. Cox, *Thomas Hardy: The Critical Heritage*. [London: Routledge, 2001], pp. 319-22).

7   The *Pall Mall Gazette* described *Jude the Obscure* as 'dirt, drivel and damnation', while Edmund Gosse, Hardy's friend and one of the first to appreciate his poetic genius, dismissed it as 'grimy' and 'indecent'. In his 1912 Postscript to his original Preface to *Jude*, Hardy wrote that 'it was to be burnt by a bishop – probably in his despair at not being able to burn me'. *Jude the Obscure* (London: Macmillan, 1966), p. vi.

8   Apology for *Late Lyrics and Earlier* (1922), *CP*, p. 532.

9   Ibid., p. 531.

Thought leads Hardy into what often seems like the darkest fatalism – and yet, and yet. There is always something more. True poets – and Hardy was a poet at heart – *make* things so that there *is* hope, in spite of all. Hardy was no theologian. He was not even consistent (though perhaps few of us are). But there is always for him a light in the darkest place, though the cost of finding it may be extreme.[10] As he once famously said, in a poem entitled 'In Tenebris II', 'if way to the Better there be, it exacts a full look at the Worst.'[11] That word 'exacts' is telling – it demands, it drags us to look, and in his stories and poems he cuts no corners off life's capacity to make us suffer. And then we come to the ageing Hardy in a little poem written in 1915, not long after the death of his first wife and his complex, guilt-ridden grieving process for the woman he had once loved, and then in later years neglected. He writes of Christmas Eve, thinking of the Christmas magic of his childhood. But it is not there now. Things change. And then there is a 'yet':

> So fair a fancy few would weave
> In these years! Yet, I feel,
> If someone said on Christmas Eve,
> 'Come; see the oxen kneel
>
> 'In the lonely barton by yonder coomb
> Our childhood used to know,'
> I should go with him in the gloom,
> Hoping it might be so.[12]

Hardy is always precise with words: 'Yet, I feel' – it never becomes more than that, indeterminate, deeper than anything rational. The bidding takes him back to the language and vocabulary of his Dorset childhood, long abandoned – 'barton' and 'coomb' – these words add to the distance of time, like looking down the years through a telescope from the wrong end. And then there is that last line – '*hoping* it *might*.' The possibility is as recessed as it can be. Is this faith, or desperation, or just plain nostalgia for a lost childhood? It is both less and more than all these things. It takes us to a place we all know, if we are honest, but

---

10 Even in Hardy's darkest fiction there is, perhaps, only one absolute tragedy, *The Mayor of Casterbridge*, just as Shakespeare wrote only one utterly tragic play, *Timon of Athens*. See, George Steiner, 'A Note on Absolute Tragedy', *Literature and Theology*, Vol. 4, No. 2 (July, 1990), 148.

11 *CP*, p. 154. Hardy quotes the line in his 'Apology' for 'Late Lyrics and Earlier', *CP*, p. 527.

12 *CP*, p. 439.

few of us have managed to express it quite so perfectly as Hardy, or even thought to do so. It is where, if *I* am honest, so often my theology painfully begins.

I said at the beginning that my love affair with poetry began when I was about thirteen, and it was with reading one of Hardy's very early poems, written in 1867, called 'Neutral Tones'. This dark poem haunts much of his fiction from *A Pair of Blue Eyes* (1873) onwards, those novels with all their blighted love affairs. It was an odd poem to attract a young boy who had not, at that stage, even felt he had fallen in love with a girl, though he tried to imagine what it would be like. But that, in reality was still a year or two off. Here is Hardy's poem, in all its starkness:

We stood by a pond that winter day,
And the sun was white, as though chidden of God.
And a few leaves lay on the starving sod;
    They had fallen from an ash and were gray.

Your eyes on me were as eyes that rove
Over tedious riddles of years ago;
And some words played between us to and fro
    On which lost the more by our love.

The smile on your mouth was the deadest thing
Alive enough to have strength to die;
And a grin of bitterness swept thereby
    Like an ominous bird a-wing. . .

Since then, keen lessons that love deceives,
And wrings with wrong, have shaped to me
Your face, and the God-curst sun, and a tree,
    And a pond edged with grayish leaves.[13]

I can still hardly read that poem without tears. Thomas Hardy has, I think, the finest ear of any poet I know. By that I mean that it is virtually impossible to find a line in all the thousands of his *Collected Poems* (and by no means all of his poems are anywhere nearly as good as 'Neutral Tones') that does not scan perfectly, does not make beautiful music in the rhythm of words, often simple and perfectly turned, as Mozart turns musical notes. It is a divine gift. 'Neutral Tones' is an elegy about the end of a love affair. The point is that it is no-one's fault, no-one is morally

---

13 *CP*, p. 9.

responsible, the love has just died. God is mentioned twice – the cold sun is bleached white 'as though chidden of God', a sun that is later 'God-curst'. The images haunt us – the dead, hopeless smile that comforts no-one, 'alive enough to have strength to die'. There is no enmity – nothing. Hardy, without being morbid, was fascinated with what it must feel like to be dead – an obsession never stronger than after the death of his first wife Emma, as he goes back over the years and seeks to rediscover their first, glorious love affair in Cornwall, now lost in time. 'Neutral Tones' has a precise sense of place – Hardy *sees* the world in detail, picking out the details we notice when we can see no way forward. He knows the world as the place of human suffering, noting the sun, the graying leaves, the tree, the pond, the remembered face that are all part of the situation. And it is no-one's fault. It just is, and nothing can be done about it: 'love deceives and wrings with wrong.' That word 'wrings' is perfect, making us pause and fumble for its meaning for a moment.

There are no simple answers in Hardy's world. But he can never quite leave it there in confusion. With all his fatalism and pessimistic tendencies, Hardy retains a profound sense of life's persistence and its capacity to survive in the simple eternities of human existence. All his life he hated war, its wastefulness and purposelessness, and in 1915 he wrote one of his greatest poems, entitled 'In Time of "The Breaking of Nations"'. As so often in Hardy's verse, it is deceptively simple, celebrating the profound consistencies of life that survive the passing enormities of human conflict: the sleepy ploughman, smoke from burning cut grass . . . and love. As always he reverts in these moments to the Dorset vocabulary of his youth:

> Yonder a maid and her wight
>   Come whispering by:
> War's annals will cloud into night
>   Ere their story die.[14]

Hardy is never cynical, for the true poet knows that cynicism is cheap. Simple words, used precisely, become portals into deeper truths: 'Come whispering by' – that word 'whispering' brings the couple to life, speaking their own language that is not for our ears, saying that which remains for us unsaid. The next line picks up the image of the 'clouds of war' that gather and then pass – 'cloud into night'. Writing of this young, universal couple, Hardy, perhaps, was thinking of himself as a

---

14 *CP*, p. 511.

young man in love with Emma Gifford in their first, fine moments of romance in north Cornwall, while we, each one of us, thinks of . . . I leave that to each of you. For Thomas and Emma at Castle Boterel, the ancient, primaeval rocks beside the road that have stood for millennia record nothing except – 'that we two passed'.[15] Such moments are eternal. Here Hardy challenges us with a profound simplicity that is something like that which we have come to call, after Paul Ricoeur, a second naïveté.[16] Hardy never underestimates the significance of those instances of vision that lie at the heart of life's deepest realities – he was, after all, a deeply religious man who could be angry at the hide-bound formalities of the church – the church that would not baptise Tess Durbeyfield's baby because it was born out of wedlock – and who stood up to what he perceived as the cruelty of God with stark defiance. (Hardy had no time for that question of theodicy, over which Milton pondered for the twelve books of *Paradise Lost*. How can we sustain a belief in a loving and all-powerful God in a world of evil? Hardy cannot sustain such a belief.) But he returns time and again to that 'something' that is too often lost in philosophical reflection, something, what shall we say, more 'religious', which may or may not have to do with God? In his poem 'Afternoon Service at Mellstock' he goes back to Dorset in 1850, when he would have been ten years old, an untutored lad of working class parents:

On afternoons of drowsy calm
    We stood in the panelled pew,
Singing one-voiced a Tate-and-Brady psalm
    To the tune of 'Cambridge New.'

We watched the elms, we watched the rooks,
    The clouds upon the breeze,
Between the whiles of glancing at our books,
    And swaying like the trees.

So mindless were those outpourings!
    Though I am not aware
That I have gained by subtle thought on things
    Since we stood psalming there.[17]

---

15 'At Castle Boterel', *CP*, p. 331.
16 See, Paul Ricoeur, *The Symbolism of Evil*, trans. by Emerson Buchanan (Boston: Beacon Press, 1969).
17 *CP*. p. 403.

It is a marvelous poem. The children have no idea what they are singing about in the Tate-and-Brady psalm, sung to the tune of *Cambridge New*. It is that second verse of the poem that captures the moment. They are gazing out of the windows of the church, as children do, merely glancing at their books – but they 'watched' the elms, the rooks, the clouds. . .. and so, without thinking, becoming themselves in their watching one with nature even to their swaying like trees in the wind. 'So mindless were those outpourings' – these outpourings are not of the intellect, but from somewhere deeper, less conscious, and more lasting in the end. This is where the religious spirit begins, more than in any 'subtle thought'. It was not enough to keep Hardy in the Church of England, with its pomp and circumstance and corruption, but he remains yet one of the most God-haunted poets I know.

Hardy came from humble stock and received a modest education at a school in Dorchester before becoming a pupil in a provincial architect's office. He never went to University (though he was to receive five honorary degrees in later life), but was, as he is described by his second wife Florence (though the words are possibly his own), 'a born bookworm',[18] not afraid to tackle the most difficult of texts from Hegel to, at the end of his life, Albert Einstein and relativity theory, on which he commented with some understanding. Whilst writing one of his darkest novels, *The Woodlanders* (1885), he was reading the philosopher Hegel, noting that, 'philosophers seem to start wrong; they cannot get away from a prepossession that the world must somehow have been made to be a comfortable place for man.'[19] For Hardy, the world was anything but comfortable, though there was joy still to be found. Readers of *Tess of the D'Urbervilles* are familiar from the novel's last page with the Aeschylean President of the Immortals who plays with poor Tess even to her death for his mere sport (Hardy might also have been thinking of the gods in Gloucester's words in Act IV of *King Lear* who kill us for their sport, we being 'like flies to wanton boys'), or the indifferent, mechanical Immanent Will of Hardy's last great work *The Dynasts* (1904-8):

> It works unconsciously, as heretofore,
> Eternal artistries in Circumstances,

---

18 Florence Hardy, *The Life of Thomas Hardy* (*The Early Life*, 1928) (London: Studio Editions, 1994), p. 35.

19 Quoted in Claire Tomalin, *Thomas Hardy: The Time-Torn Man.* (London: Viking, 2006), p. 223.

Whose patterns, wrought by rapt aesthetic rote,
Seem in themselves Its single listless aim,
And not their consequence.[20]

But more intense than either of these is Hardy's sense of the seeming
cruelty and callous forgetfulness of the personal God of his Christian
upbringing. In his poem 'God's Education', Hardy challenges the God
who brings upon us old age, extinguishing the light and beauty of
youth. Age comes upon us cruelly and imperceptibly, and the lovely
young woman grows old:

I saw him steal the light away
    That haunted in her eye:
It went so gently none could say
More than that it was there one day
    And missing by-and-by.

I watched her longer, and he stole
    Her lily tincts and rose;
All her young sprightliness of soul
Next fell beneath his cold control,
    And disappeared like those.

I asked: 'Why do you serve her so?
    Do you, for some glad day,
Hoard these her sweets−?' He said, 'O no,
They charm not me; I bid Time throw
    Them carelessly away.'

Said I: 'We call that cruelty -
    We, your poor mortal kind.'
He mused. 'The thought is new to me.
Forsooth, though I men's master be,
    Theirs is the teaching mind!'[21]

As always Hardy's perfect control of his verse reflects every shade
of feeling. The thumping fourth line of the second stanza hammers
home its iron point. 'All her young sprightliness of soul/Next fell
beneath his cold control/And disappeared. . . .' In the end it is the

---

20 Thomas Hardy, *The Dynasts: An Epic-Drama.* (London: Macmillan, 1965), p.
    1.
21 *CP,* p. 261.

poet who speaks to God, who 'educates' Him upon the meaning of cruelty. What is the point of all this decay and loss? God answers that there is no point, but simply 'they charm me not'. God is indifferent, though the poet gives that a moral twist and calls that cruelty – God's cruelty. We are back to the world of 'Neutral Tones' with which I began – a morally indifferent world in which any moral teaching is from humankind to God, not the other way around. Hardy is no implied theologian like John Milton who sets out in *Paradise Lost* to 'justify the ways of God to men'. That is another story, though as one perceptive critic has said of Milton's great epic poem, in it God is finally justified, after the Fall, in ways that might have surprised even Him in a triumph of Renaissance humanism.[22] Quite simply, after the Fall, Adam and Eve grow up and become responsible adults. But Hardy, in a different and perhaps harsher age, cannot go even thus far. His pessimism can plumb the depths. In 1889 he noted that 'this planet does not supply the materials for happiness to higher existences [meaning human beings]. Other planets may, though one can hardly see how.'[23] And yet . . . that is never quite the end of the story.

Although Christ is mentioned very rarely in Hardy's poems and novels, his whole life is, in a sense, the writing of a Passion of mankind, a following of humanity into the abyss to discover there an insistent, ineradicable vitality that throws out a challenge to the cruelty of God, and somehow can never quite be free of the possibility of something more – hoping it might be so. Hardy, in his times, cries out again and again, against the God who has forsaken him and perhaps the point is that it is precisely here, where theology seems helpless and pointless, that the challenge to it is most acute; where, in a way, we start becoming theological. We all too often prefer our comfort zones, sometimes abandoning them when they fail us. Not so Hardy. As an old man Hardy continues to feel that 'sprightliness of soul' that his decaying body seems to belie. (Photographs of him as an old man in the 1920s reveal a face that, with all its tragedy, can yet see the funny side of old age. And he was quite capable of falling for a pretty female face to the very end, rather to the understandable distress of both his first and second wife):

---

22 David Daiches, *God and the Poets* (Oxford: Clarendon Press, 1984), p. 49.

23 Quoted in Tomalin, op. cit. p. 224.

I look into my glass,
And view my wasting skin,
And say, 'Would God it came to pass
My heart had shrunk as thin!'

For then, I, undistrest
By hearts grown cold to me,
Could lonely wait my endless rest
With equanimity.

But Time, to make me grieve,
Part steals, let part abide;
And shakes this fragile frame at eve
With throbbings of noontide.[24]

As so often, Hardy catches the complexity of that all too familiar moment. There is no equanimity. An energy, indeed a sexual drive, remains within the old man's frame as he catches his face in the mirror, as we all do, or will if we are spared, and thinks, 'is that old face really me . . .?'. For the heart is young, and nowhere is this dilemma more tragically, delicately, beautifully caught than in the poems he wrote after the death of his first wife Emma in November 1912.

Theirs had been a romantic wooing in a remote, wild part of north Cornwall forty years previously. But the marriage had outworn itself and in their later years they were almost estranged, having run out of both conversation and mutual comfort. It was said that Emma became mad, but I could never see that her undoubted eccentricities went that far. She just lost her way, and Hardy had no use for her. There was unkindness on both sides. And when Emma died, the poet in Hardy met full on the complexities of what had become indeed one of life's tragedies. In *Poems of 1912-13* he goes back in time to recover a lost love, and he actually did physically return to Cornwall to 'find' his Emma again. In these extraordinary poems Emma lives once more, a 'ghost-girl-rider' galloping along the Cornish cliffs with bright hair flapping free.[25] Of course wrongs done cannot finally be undone if they remain unforgiven before death, and so what was Hardy looking for in these poems that are among some of the most beautiful in the English language? It was a making, or rather a re-making of a world – a recovery of a human love that had been real

---

24 *CP*. p. 72.
25 'The Phantom Horsewoman', 'Beeny Cliff', *CP*, pp. 333, 330

and powerful before the world and human nature trampled on it. There is tragedy in these poems but also something intensely alive, real, beautiful, even gladsome. As a young boy of thirteen, when I read these poems for the first time (and most of them I can still recite in full by heart) I encountered something so powerful that I doubt if any theology or theological account of the world I have read since can come anywhere near to matching it: and that 'something' remains with me – impossible, real – meaning what to my rather too comfortable 'religious' self in older age? In 'The Phantom Horsewoman' Hardy looks at himself in the third person simply as 'a man I know'. We all do that from time to time, telling our story through the lens of 'someone I know', though it is really ourselves. It helps to distance things that are too painful:

> Queer are the ways of a man I know:
> > He comes and stands
> > In a careworn craze,
> > And looks at the sands
> > And the seaward haze
> > With moveless hands,
> > And face and gaze,
> > Then turns to go. . .
> And what does he see when he gazes so?[26]

The second stanza begins with a device familiar enough to all of us again as we speak of the world at large or people in general – 'They say . . .'. Hardy makes himself into, or perhaps, indeed, he was, one of those dotty old people whose gaze is not quite focussed, not quite 'with us' – though what he sees in the distant past is perfectly precise, 'an instant thing/More clear than to-day'. Hardy knows that Emma is no longer real, but what is reality, after all? He has an extraordinary sense of emotional recollection and in his imagination she is almost alive and as she was so that 'Time touches her not.'[27]

---

26 *CP*, p. 332.

27 This power of emotional recollection was, to a degree, also in Emma herself. Her autobiographical writings entitled *Some Recollections*, which ends with their marriage on 'a perfect September day' in 1874, has been published and its importance for Hardy himself is clear. As Robert Gittings has written, 'Immeasurably the greater writer, Hardy achieves a poetic intensity beyond Emma's aim or ability; but his debt to her is clear for all to see.' Introduction to Emma Hardy, *Some Recollections*, ed. by Evelyn Hardy and Robert Gittings

What do we do with this? It is easy to dismiss it all as the fanciful imaginings of an old man who had not been a very good husband and whose conscience was troubling him, even as his heart breaks for a past that cannot be retrieved. But there is much more to this extraordinary poetry than just this. Something more is happening. Here is perhaps the greatest of the *Poems of 1912-13*, 'The Voice'. It has to be read in full:

Woman much missed, how you call to me, call to me,
Saying that now you are not as you were
When you had changed from the one who was all to me,
But as at first, when our day was fair.

Can it be you that I hear? Let me view you, then,
Standing as when I drew near to the town
Where you would wait for me: yes, as I knew you then,
Even to the original air-blue gown!

Or is it only the breeze, in its listlessness
Travelling across the wet mead to me here,
You being ever dissolved to wan wistlessness,
Heard no more again far or near?

    Thus I; faltering forward,
    Leaves around me falling,
Wind oozing thin through the thorn from norward,
    And the woman calling.[28]

Let me just clear up one thing first. Hardy changed the last line of the second stanza. In the first version it reads, 'Even to the original hat and gown', and he altered it to the wonderful, wonderfully-sounding, and precise image of 'the original air-blue gown', that haunts the mind and the imagination.

The poem is a reliving of a present experience that is intensely felt and known as the recovery of a moment in time that is long past. The agony is felt in the first line, for Emma is gone – 'Woman much missed . . .'. – her call heard *now* already fading on the air in the repeated 'call to me, call to me'. Already she is slipping away, and the first three stanzas are a precise act of the imagination as the moment recedes as quickly as it came and cannot be held. It is at its most intense at the beginning of the second stanza. Not satisfied with the hearing of the voice (it is already fading and is it actually *her* anyway?), the sound must become also a vision demanded in the words, 'Let me view you, then.' The present has to coincide exactly with the past – 'yes, as I knew you, then' – and for just a moment the appearance becomes real, almost tangible, within the verse in that glimpsed 'air-blue gown' – remembered as we remember such things and such moments as they come to us once in a lifetime. Just for an instant, as in all true love, and in the words of another poet, Louis MacNeice, 'time was away and she was here'[29] – and past and present are one in that instant. But then the doubts creep in. In the last stanza of 'The Voice' the shape and rhythm of the verse deliberately fall apart, like the old poet himself, stumbling and 'faltering forward'. The glamour of the moment is gone as the old man staggers amidst the leaves and the north wind – 'and the woman calling'. But is she still there in spite of all, or a ghost, or a figment of his imagination? The dream never quite leaves him.

Another of these remarkable poems begins with the lines 'I found her out there/On a slope few see.' It is that word 'found' that is so troubling. Does it refer to that glorious moment when, as a young man, Thomas Hardy on a professional visit from London 'found' Emma in remote Cornwall and fell in love with her, or to the aged Hardy revisiting old haunts after her death in 1912 when he finds her ghost lingering in his memory? He wants to believe – oh, how he wants to believe. But there is always hesitancy, and he knows in the end that she is no longer there. And yet, and yet: the last stanza begins again with insistent hope . . . maybe:

> Yet her shade, maybe,
> Will creep underground
> Till it catch the sound
> Of that western sea
> As it swells and sobs
> Where she once domiciled
> And joy in its throbs
> With the heart of a child.[30]

Hardy's poetry can be heart-breaking, but for all its absorption, it is rarely self-indulgent or merely nostalgic. It is too serious and too precise for that. In spite of all his pessimism and his imperfections

29 Louis MacNeice, 'Meeting Point', (https://www.poetryfoundation.org/poems/91396/meeting-point).

30 *CP*, p. 322.

as man and as a husband – like the rest of us he could be vain and contradictory, selfish and thoughtless, and deeply insecure in spite of all his fame and fortune in life – his poetic gift creates a world that still – in spite of all – inspires hope, however dim and against reason, and celebrates the joy and vitality of life even when these gifts can seem a burden to an old and dying man. In the early years of the twentieth century Hardy was writing at a time when intellectuals and writers were fascinated by the French philosopher Henri Bergson and his notion of *élan vital* (Bergson's book *Creative Evolution*, where this phrase was coined, was published in 1907, translated into English in 1911, and had a profound effect on many writers including Nikos Kazantzakis, Marcel Proust and Thomas Mann), or were struggling with the ideas of Friedrich Nietzsche – but for me, Hardy's poetry offers something rather different and in its way more complex, more living, more immediate.

Time and again, and above all in *Poems of 1912-13*, Hardy goes back to a moment in a person's history that gives meaning and vitality to everything else in life. It does not guarantee that things will not go wrong, or that love cannot die (as it has done in 'Neutral Tones'), but in a moment of supreme imaginative energy, it can affirm a fundamental sense of life and even joy, such as even all of Hardy's most tragic characters in his fiction can know, if only for a moment. In another poem that takes place in Mellstock church,[31] 'A Church Romance (Mellstock: circa 1835)', Hardy relives the moment when his parents first caught sight of one another. They were not married when Thomas was conceived, and their long marriage was far from perfect though, like many others, it worked well enough. But Hardy wants us never to forget its inception in the church, his father playing the fiddle before the advent of the church organ, a development described in Hardy's early novel *Under the Greenwood Tree* (1872):

> Thus their hearts' bond began, in due time signed.
> And long years hence, when Age had scared Romance,
> At some old attitude of his or glance
> That gallery-scene would break upon her mind,
> With him as minstrel, ardent, young, and trim,
> Bowing 'New Sabbath' or 'Mount Ephraim'.[32]

---

31 'Mellstock' lies at the very heart of Hardy's Wessex, on the edge of Egdon Heath, consisting of three hamlets on the road to Casterbridge. It features in many of the novels.

32 *CP*, p. 236.

Looking at the few photographs we have of Hardy's parents – his rather handsome but weak father, and the powerful, serious mother who had been a servant maid who had known what it was to work hard physically, and it shows – the poem is all the more touching. Indeed, there was nothing very romantic in their lives, and Thomas grew away from them as he became more successful and mixed with people in a wider world outside their class. But the vision remains.

So – where is all of this leading us? Before I begin to draw to some kind of conclusion in this chapter I want to make a brief detour into another time and another poet, long after Hardy's death. When the scale and enormity of what has become known as the Holocaust – the slaughter of some six million Jews and others in eastern Europe during the Second World War – became apparent, the philosopher Theodor Adorno famously remarked that no poetry was possible in the face of such a hideous act of humanity upon its own humanity.[33] Nothing can properly be said. And indeed Christian theologians and philosophers were conspicuously silent – for how indeed was God to be justified in the face of such horror? But from the ashes words were written and spoken. They were the words of the poets – above all the survivor Paul Celan, seeking to recover his identity as a Jew and his language, which was German. Celan is one of the greatest poets of the twentieth century. It did not save him personally from despair – he died a suicide's death – but his poetry is a remarkable effusion of life from the very midst of death. Perhaps his greatest poem, and certainly the best known – *Todesfuge*, or 'Death Fugue' – is a quite extraordinary lament for the Jewish people, rooted in Jewish scripture, but grounded also in the German poet Goethe and the musical rhythms of Bach's unfinished and supremely beautiful *Art of Fugue*. In death the poem is a great statement of life. The poet, art, speaks into life.

I use this illustration because Thomas Hardy's great achievement was to render life in words, sometimes from the darkness of deep despair. Even poor Michael Henchard, in his death at the end of *The Mayor of Casterbridge*, gains, paradoxically, a degree of immortality in the language of his terrible, self-negating will, and out of love for him and his words Elizabeth-Jane holds onto the paper on which his will is written even as she tries to be faithful to this will, 'a piece of the same stuff his whole life was made of':

---

33 Rowan Williams has pointed out that, more strictly, Adorno is talking about the 'barbarity' of writing poetry after Auschwitz. See, *The Edge of Words: God and the Habits of Language*. (London: Bloomsbury, 2014), p. 159.

That Elizabeth-Jane Farfrae be not told of my death, or made to
grieve on account of me.
& that I be not bury'd in consecrated ground.
& that no sexton be asked to toll the bell.
& that nobody is wished to see my dead body.
& that no murners walk behind me at my funeral.
& that no flours be planted on my grave.
& that no man remember me.
To this I put my name.
Michael Henchard[34]

Rarely have words been so powerful, or words of forgetting been so
memorable. Hardy as a poet knew the power of the living word. Like many
poets, he was less articulate when he tried to explain or analyse things. He
was no philosopher or theologian – though he seems to have read much
theology, but with a poet's eye. After a literary gathering in 1904, Arthur
Benson, the son of an Archbishop of Canterbury and a Cambridge don,
wrote on Hardy's understanding of the great Cardinal John Henry Newman:

> Hardy talked rather interestingly of Newman; he has read the
> *Apologia*, & I *thought* he said 'I joined the RC Church for
> a time, but it has left no impression whatever on me now.'
> [This was certainly *not* the case! DJ] Then he said very firmly
> that Newman was no logician; that the *Apologia* was simply
> a poet's work, with a kind of lattice-work of logic in places to
> screen the poetry.[35]

If these are, indeed, Hardy's words, then they are actually a rather good
comment on Newman's *Apologia Pro Vita Sua*. Newman was, after all,
himself a poet as well as a theologian, though he was far from reaching
the poetic status of Hardy himself.

Hardy's poetry sets us in precise and difficult places and against these
we may, perhaps, test the validity of our religious views, positions and
affirmations. Only once, as far as I know, does Hardy actually write at any
length about poetry and religion, in his 1922 Introduction to the collection
of poems entitled *Late Lyrics and Earlier*. It is an interesting moment,
typically Hardy becoming rather clumsy when he attempts to be a critic:

---

34 Thomas Hardy, *The Mayor of Casterbridge* [1886] (London: Macmillan, 1966), p.
    333.

35 Quoted in Tomalin, op. cit. p. 284, from the diary of Arthur Benson, 30 April
    1904, Magdalene College, Cambridge.

> In any event poetry, pure literature in general, religion – I
> include religion, in its essential and undogmatic sense,
> because poetry and religion touch each other, or rather
> modulate into each other; are, indeed, often but different
> names for the same thing – these, I say, the visible signs of
> mental and emotional life, must like all other things keep
> moving, becoming.[36]

Then, in this Introduction, like most old men, Hardy breaks into a
lament for the present time, when things seem to be moving backwards
rather than forwards. He speaks of the church, both the Roman Catholic
Church and the Church of England, each of them having had their
chance to move forward, but neither having succeeded in doing so, the
latter typically losing the opportunity for renewal in what Hardy calls
'the hesitating English instinct towards liturgical reform (a flank march
which I at the time quite expected to witness, with the gathering of
many millions of waiting agnostics into its fold.)'[37] But the Church of
England lost its chance again, though Hardy is irritatingly imprecise in
his reference here. He has little hope in the churches for the future. But
then he concludes on a poetic note, admitting that he is an old man who
does not see things quite so clearly:

> It may be a forlorn hope, a mere dream, that of an alliance
> between religion, which must be retained unless the world is
> to perish, and complete rationality, which must come, unless
> also the world is to perish, by means of the interfusing effect
> of poetry – 'the breath and finer spirit of all knowledge; the
> impassioned expression of science', as it was defined by an
> English poet.[38]

(The poet is, of course, William Wordsworth.) But what of that phrase
about 'the interfusing effect of poetry'? I wonder how far that is felt,
let alone its importance realised, today. If I have done nothing else
in this chapter, I hope that I have shown how Hardy makes us *see*
the world in a more alert way: how those moments that define our
lives, especially those which define them for the better, should be
held in the imagination, to shed a light and become places in which

---

36 *CP*, p. 530.
37 Ibid., p. 531.
38 Ibid.

meaning and coherence might begin to be formed and then reformed. Theologians, like philosophers, as we have seen in Hardy's words, have an incorrigible habit of 'starting wrong' – beginning in the wrong place and claiming too much too quickly. Hardy's poetry rarely judges – I began with 'Neutral Tones', a poem that offers no moral condemnation at the end of the affair. Is this pure fatalism? Do we just have to accept that that is just how things are and so we must put up with it, as seems to be the case at the end of *The Mayor of Casterbridge*, in Elizabeth-Jane's words, 'But there's no altering – so it must be.'[39] Or is it an opportunity to start again, however laboriously and painfully, having learnt something from life's 'keen lessons'. Let me finish with a little known poem by Hardy that is also a kind of short story. It is called 'At the Railway Station, Upway'.[40] What does it mean? Or rather, what does it tell us? And what difference does it make to us – as Christians, or perhaps just more plainly as human beings? We wonder at Hardy's economy of words – words not to be wasted as he builds up a whole world for us in half a page of verse:

> 'There is not much that I can do,
>   For I've no money that's quite my own!'
>   Spoke up the pitying child –
> A little boy with a violin
> At the station before the train came in, -
> 'But I can play my fiddle to you,
> And a nice one 'tis, and good in tone!'
>
> The man in the handcuffs smiled;
> The constable looked, and he smiled, too,
>   As the fiddle began to twang;
> And the man in the handcuffs suddenly sang
>   With grimful glee:
>   'This life so free
>   Is the thing for me!'
>
> And the constable smiled and said no word,
> As if unconscious of what he heard;
> And so they went on till the train came in –
> The convict, and boy with the violin.

---

39 Thomas Hardy, *The Mayor of Casterbridge*. (London: Macmillan, 1966), p. 333.
40 *CP*, p. 575.

Hardy played the violin as a boy, playing at dances with his father, who, as we have seen, used to play in 'Mellstock' (actually Stinsford) church before the organ arrived and the minstrels were disbanded. Even in old age he still played from time to time – and I wonder if this poem is, in fact, based on an incident in his own life. Perhaps. But it is beautifully realised, with its levels of irony, its innocence, and above all in what remains unsaid.

On the day before he died in 1928, Thomas Hardy asked his second wife Florence to read a verse from Fitzgerald's *Omar Khayyám* to him:

> Oh, Thou, who Man of baser Earth didst make
> And who with Eden didst devise the Snake;
> For all the Sin wherewith the Face of Man
> Is blacken'd, Man's Forgiveness give – and take![41]

He is back in the realm of the poem 'God's Education' – at the bitter end we need God's forgiveness – but does God also need ours? Does God need to be educated by us? Yet these are not Hardy's absolutely final moments. The next day, his sister-in-law Eva was with him when apparently, after some rambling words, he asked, with some curiosity, 'Eva, what is this?'[42] It was death approaching. Even here, the poet was, agnostic, curious to know. The question remained unanswered.

In the next chapter I turn to one of the great religious thinkers of the nineteenth century, the poet Samuel Taylor Coleridge.

---

41 Quoted in Tomalin, op. cit. p. 369.
42 Ibid.

Samuel Taylor Coleridge
(1772-1834)

3.
Samuel Taylor Coleridge:
Words as Living Things

If Thomas Hardy was my first love in English poetry, then Samuel Taylor Coleridge (1772-1834), whom I encountered very much later, was certainly my second love, so much so that I devoted my doctoral studies at the University of Durham entirely to him, eventually joining the vast ranks of Coleridge critics by writing a book about him on the subject of poetry and religion, mine being entitled *Coleridge as Poet and Religious Thinker* (1985). Coleridge on language and faith continues to feature prominently in my last book but one, and certainly my most autobiographical, *Literature and Theology as a Grammar of Assent* (2016).

Actually Coleridge was not all that much of a poet, it seems to me, except for a few truly memorable poems such as 'Kubla Khan' and 'The Rime of the Ancient Mariner', but he was a major *thinker*, or perhaps better a contemplative, all of whose reflections are saturated with a poetic as well as a religious sensibility. He read, it seems, everything, and not only in English, such that he wrote in a letter to John Thelwall of 19 November 1796: 'I am, & ever have been, a great reader – & have read almost everything – a library-cormorant – I am *deep* in all out of the way books, whether of the monkish times, or of the puritanical aera [sic]'.[1] He was right, too. He does seem to have read everything. But what

---

1   *Collected Letters of Samuel Taylor Coleridge*, Vol. 1, 1785-1800, ed. by Earl Leslie

attracts me to Coleridge, finally, is his deep and loving respect for words and language. He regarded words as nothing less than living things, powerful to create and to destroy, to be loved and sometimes feared. His familiar definition of what he called the 'primary imagination' is that it is 'the living Power and prime Agent of all human Perception, and as a repetition in the finite mind of the eternal act of creation in the infinite I AM'.[2] There is, typically for Coleridge, so much in this brief statement. He always packed his words tightly and precisely into his sentences. We no longer value or even understand with any degree of seriousness the power and importance of the imagination as Coleridge and some of his contemporaries did, regarding it as we do now as a kind of optional extra to the real business of knowledge, something centred largely on the world of children. But Coleridge took the imagination absolutely seriously. He linked it to God's creative word at the beginning of the book of Genesis, and the poet is thus the closest to the divine and the most to be feared of all human beings. A recent scholar of Coleridge, John Coulson, a man whom I came to know and respect immensely after I had recovered from the shock of having him as my examiner in Oxford, spoke of Coleridge's language as 'fiduciary',[3] that is living and creative, refusing what Coleridge dramatically once called 'a Chaos grinding itself into compatibility'.[4] For him words were open-ended and finally mysterious.

For forty years now I have been reflecting upon and marveling at Coleridge's description of the language of the Bible as he describes it in his Lay Sermon of 1816 entitled *The Statesman's Manual: The Bible as the Best Guide to Political Skill and Foresight*. Our current crop of politicians and public figures might do well to spend some time with it. These sentences are burnt into my memory. They speak of nothing less than the power of words themselves:

> In the Scriptures they are the living *educts* of the Imagination;
> of that reconciling and mediatory power, which incorporating
> the Reason in Images of the Sense, and organizing (as it
> were) the flux of the Senses by the permanence and self-

    Griggs (Oxford: The Clarendon Press, 1966), p. 260.

2   S.T. Coleridge, *Biographia Literaria* [1817], ed. by James Engell and W. Jackson Bate. Vol 1. (Princeton: Princeton University Press, 1983), p. 304.

3   See, John Coulson, *Newman and the Common Tradition: A Study in the Language of Church and Society* (Oxford: Clarendon Press, 1970).

4   Quoted in David Jasper, *Literature and Theology as a Grammar of Assent* (Farnham: Ashgate, 2016), p. 15.

circling energies of the Reason, gives birth to a system of symbols, harmonious in themselves and consubstantial with the truths, of which they are the *conductors*. These are the Wheels which Ezekiel beheld, when the hand of the Lord was upon him, and he saw visions of God as he sate among the captives by the river of Chebar.[5]

I could spend the rest of this chapter on these dense words and images, but I prefer to let them speak for themselves – difficult, compact, challenging. These wheels, of course, refer to Ezekiel's marvelous vision (Ezekiel 1: 15-21), whose complexity Coleridge almost matches. Yet, at the same time, it is all perfectly simple. Words themselves are the vehicles, the wheels of 'the living chariot that bears up (for *us*) the throne of the Divine Humanity'. We are carried on words to Christ himself.

Part of the impetus behind writing this present book is that I fear that today we are in danger of losing this sense of the extraordinary and often elusive power of words. The language of our liturgy in church, as I have written on at length in another book,[6] is in danger of falling into the trap of utilitarianism and the misguided notion that all language must be clear and easily comprehensible, rather than something beautiful, fearful, challenging, living and creative. Coleridge is intensely aware of this. It was he who, writing about his fellow lakeland poet William Wordsworth, understood poetry as demanding nothing less than a 'poetic faith' that is 'the willing suspension of disbelief'.[7] This poetic faith requires us, then, to abandon all our skepticisms and rationalisations for something more important, and ultimately more intelligent. Coleridge is never an easy writer, poet or thinker. He wants us to reflect upon our thinking, not to assume that we know everything dogmatically from the start. Philosophically it is hardly surprising that he was one of the first English readers of the philosopher Immanuel Kant with his incessant demand that we reflect upon epistemology – the business of continually thinking about how we think, and of how we come to know.

Oddly one of things I rather like about Coleridge is that he was, in a sense and in the eyes of much of the world, a total seeming failure. He was what we would now probably describe as a drug addict – hooked

---

5   S.T. Coleridge, *Lay Sermons*, ed. by R.J. White (Princeton: Princeton University Press, 1972), pp. 28-9.

6   David Jasper, *The Language of Liturgy: A Ritual Poetics* (London: SCM, 2018)

7   *Biographia Literaria*, Vol. 2, p. 6.

on laudanum which was a medicinal tincture based in opium – a dreadful hypochondriac who never really earned an honest living, a literary prevaricator, and finally he was certainly pretty much a failure as a family man. He had an enormous capacity for falling out with people and especially his closest friends – and so we might conclude he was pretty much of a dead loss. But still he was rather wonderful. Here is Thomas Carlyle's description of Coleridge in his last years when he lodged on Highgate Hill outside London in the house of his doctor Mr Gilman:

> Coleridge sat on the brow of Highgate Hill, in those years, looking down on London and its smoke-tumult, like a sage escaped from the inanity of life's battle; attracting towards him the thoughts of innumerable brave souls still engaged there, . . . a kind of prophetic or magician character. . . .
>
> A sublime man; who, alone in those dark days had saved his crown of spiritual manhood; escaping from the black materialisms, and revolutionary deluges, with 'God, Freedom, Immortality' still his: a king of men. The practical intellects of the world did not much heed him, or carelessly reckoned him a metaphysical dreamer: but to the rising spirits of the young generation he had this dusky sublime character; and sat there, as a kind of *Magus*, girt in mystery and enigma; his Dodona oak-grove (Mr Gilman's house at Highgate) whispering strange things, uncertain whether oracles or jargon.[8]

Coleridge would not do well in today's world, but then he did not do well in his own either. Yet the more perceptive of the younger generation in his day saw something in him. Without founding any school of thought or poetry, his influence upon the nineteenth century was profound, not least upon that secretive Cambridge intellectual society known as the Cambridge Apostles, who were, in their time, profoundly to influence the poets and writers of the Bloomsbury Group.[9] More theologically and circumspectly, Cardinal John Henry Newman wrote of Coleridge in his *Apologia Pro Vita Sua* (1864):

---

8   Thomas Carlyle, *The Life of John Sterling* [1851], in *Selected Writings*, ed. by Alan Shelston (Harmondsworth: Penguin, 1971), p. 315.

9   See, Peter Allen, *The Cambridge Apostles* (Cambridge: Cambridge University Press, 1978).

While history in prose and verse was thus made the instrument of Church feelings and opinions, a philosophical basis for the same was laid in England by a very original thinker, who, while he indulged a liberty of speculation, which no Christian can tolerate, and advocated conclusions which were often heathen rather than Christian, yet after all installed a higher philosophy into inquiring minds, than they had hitherto been accustomed to accept. In this way he made trial of his age.[10]

Coleridge was a poet with a profound philosophical sensibility, capable of influencing even those whose religious views diverged wildly from his own, and perhaps especially devout Christians like Newman. In his later years it is difficult to ascertain very precisely what Coleridge's religious position as regards Christianity was, though a less critical admirer than Newman, the dour Scottish theologian John Tulloch, described Coleridge as a 'spiritual genius' in the tradition of Richard Hooker and John Milton,[11] placing his thought at the very heart of nineteenth theological reflection. And yet it has to be admitted that, though the son of an Anglican clergyman, Coleridge had little real love for the church or for parsons, famously, when faced with the baptism of his son Hartley, asserting that he would not 'suffer the Toad of Priesthood to spurt out his foul juice in this Babe's face . . . while the fat paw of a Parson cross his forehead'.[12] He did not mince his words.

Yet Coleridge, for all such strong assertions, was undeniably a deeply religious man, but best understood, perhaps, as a religious *thinker* more than anything else.[13]

So what of his poetry? I admit that I rather struggle with the poems up to about 1798, when Coleridge was twenty seven. He himself describes his early long philosophical poem, 'Religious Musings' (1794), a hotch-potch of his ideas to date after the French Revolution, as 'Elaborate & swelling – but the Heart/Not owns it' [sic].[14] That

---

10 J.H. Newman, *Apologia Pro Vita Sua* [1864], ed. by Ian Ker (Harmondsworth: Penguin, 1994), p. 100.

11 John Tulloch, *Movements of Religious Thought in Britain During the Nineteenth Century* [1885] (Leicester: Leicester University Press, 1971), pp. 7-8 .

12 Letter to William Godwin, September 22, 1800, *Collected Letters*, Vol. 1, p. 625.

13 Hence the title of my book, *Coleridge as Poet and Religious Thinker* (London: Macmillan, 1985), and the earlier book by James D. Boulger, *Coleridge as Religious Thinker* (New Haven: Yale University Press, 1961).

14 Quoted in Richard Holmes, *Coleridge: Early Visions* (London: Hodder & Stoughton, 1989), p. 86.

describes the early poetry well – it is sometimes clever but it is, in the end, very much of a standard eighteenth century fare, and mostly rather dry and indigestible. It lacks heart. But then, later, Coleridge's verse becomes simpler and more spontaneous, partly the result perhaps of his friendship with William Wordsworth and their collaboration in *The Lyrical Ballads* (1798). The first time I really heard and felt Coleridge's poetic 'voice' was when I read 'Frost at Midnight' (1798), one of his so-called Conversation Poems, and his reflection on his schooling at Christ's Hospital in London, 'pent 'mid cloisters dim', with his hope that his son Hartley would escape this grim urban fate and become instead a child of nature. The poem begins and ends with the 'secret ministry' of the frost, exercised magically in the closing lines of the poem:

> Whether the eave-drops fall
> Heard only in the trances of the blast,
> Or if the secret ministry of frost
> Shall hang them up in silent icicles,
> Quietly shining to the quiet Moon.[15]

That final image is simply miraculous, a conversation in nature and its 'ministry' for the education of his child.

Coleridge's relationship with Christianity was profound but always difficult to pin down. Scholars continue to disagree about it. For a while as a young man he was a Unitarian preacher, and briefly edited, in 1796, a radical Christian journal called *The Watchman*. But it was always in *words* – words living and creative – that he was absorbed and by them he was himself enlivened. In a surviving fragment of a theological lecture, probably written in 1795, he anticipates a central image in 'Frost at Midnight', of the language of divinity in nature, writing that, 'We see our God everywhere – the Universe in the most literal sense in his written Language.'[16] But now see what these words and this image became in his slightly later poetry:

> so shalt thou see and hear
> The lovely shapes and sounds intelligible
> Of that eternal language, which thy God

---

15 Samuel Taylor Coleridge, *Poetical Works*, ed. by Ernest Hartley Coleridge (Oxford: Oxford University Press, 1969), p. 242.

16 S.T. Coleridge, *Lectures 1795 on Politics and Religion*, ed. by Lewis Patton and Peter Mann (Princeton: Princeton University Press, 1971), p. 339.

> Utters, who from eternity doth teach
> Himself in all, and all things in himself.[17]

It is, of course, a language that begins in Genesis, at the very beginning of the Bible, and no-one in English literature is more sensitive to it in poetry than Samuel Taylor Coleridge. His best expression of such poetic language, his most trembling awareness of it, is in his great poetic fragment 'Kubla Khan', which is by far his greatest poem. The supposed circumstances of its origin have even given a word to the *Oxford English Dictionary* – 'porlock': of one who interrupts on a matter of business. The poet has a dream and, upon waking, is about to commit it to writing. But then he is interrupted, as we read in the prose preface to the poem:

> At this moment he was unfortunately called out by a person on business from Porlock, and detained by him above an hour, and on his return to his room, found to his no small surprise and mortification, that though he still retained some vague and dim recollection of the general purport of the vision, yet, with the exception of some eight or ten scattered lines and images, all the rest had passed away.[18]

This may or may not be a description of an actual event, but those recovered and remembered eight or ten lines and images, seeing reality, as it were, through a glass darkly, are some of the most sublime in all English poetry. They speak finally of the poet – that most satanic yet also most divine of beings – recreating in words in his or her finite mind the eternal act of creation in the infinite I AM, trespassing on the very territory of God himself in the act of creation. The poet takes us back to the Garden before the Fall:

> And all who heard should see them there,
> And all should cry, Beware! Beware!
> His flashing eyes, his floating hair!
> Weave a circle round him thrice,
> And close your eyes with holy dread,
> For he on honey-dew hath fed,
> And drunk the milk of Paradise.[19]

---

17 *Poetical Works*, p. 242.
18 S.T. Coleridge, Prefatory words to 'Kubla Khan, or, A Vision in a Dream. A Fragment', *Poetical Works*, p. 296.
19 'Kubla Khan', *Poetical Works*, p. 298.

No wonder Coleridge had no time for the second-hand, rule bound maunderings of the Anglican parsons of his day. Here was indeed a priestly voice to be feared and loved.

As to second-hand maunderings, there can be few poems in English that have attracted so much commentary, a great deal of which is simply nonsense: I am writing, of course, of 'The Rime of the Ancient Mariner'. Is it an allegory, a symbol, a poem about poetry, a parable of Christian skepticism – the list of possibilities is endless. 'The Rime of the Ancient Mariner' was first published in *The Lyrical Ballads* (1798). My earliest memory of the poem is of when I heard as a schoolboy the recording of it read by Richard Burton in his glorious resonant voice with its very slight Welsh twinge – still, I think the best way to come to the poem. Poetry should be read aloud and heard. In the end, of course, like all poetry, this poem is what it is, a fabulous tale fabulously told, a fantasy of an age in which Captain Cook had only recently opened the wonders of the Pacific to western imagination, and the mutiny on HMS Bounty (1789) was still just ten years old but even yet beginning to bite into English folklore. These adventures were, in our terms today, like voyages to the moon. But then there is Coleridge's lovely riposte to Mrs Anna Laetitita Aikin Barbauld, who famously complained that *The Rime of the Ancient Mariner* lacked a moral. Mrs Barbauld was herself a moralist of a kind, and a very third rate poet whose poems return frequently to the sin of cruelty to animals, though not particularly, as far as I know, to albatrosses. Her encounter with Coleridge is recorded in his *Table Talk* for 31 March, 1832:

> Mrs. Barbauld told me that the only faults she found with the Ancient Mariner were – that it was improbable, and had no moral. As for the probability – to be sure that might admit some question – but I told her that in my judgement the chief fault of the poem was that it had too much moral, and that too openly intruded on the reader (as a principle or cause of action in a work of such pure imagination).[20]

A great deal of ink has been spilt on this remark, and I am about to spill a very little more. The first, and obvious, point to make, is that Mrs Barbauld was clearly not a woman sensitive to irony. The matter

---

20 S.T. Coleridge, *Table Talk*, Vol. 1, ed. by Carl Woodring (Princeton: Princeton University Press, 1990), pp. 272-3. The final words in brackets were added in the report of the incident in the *Quarterly Review* (August, 1834). They are in a footnote in the edition of *Table Talk* used here from the Princeton *Collected Works of Coleridge*.

of the poem's improbability I will pass by without further comment, as did Coleridge. But what of the matter of the moral and its excess in a poem of pure imagination? I am going to assume that Coleridge here is referring to the final words of the Mariner spoken to the hapless 'Wedding Guest' at the very end of the poem – a kind of sermon in brief:

> Farewell, farewell! But this I tell
> To thee, thou Wedding-Guest!
> He prayeth well, who loveth well
> Both man and bird and beast.
>
> He prayeth best, who loveth best
> All things both great and small;
> For the dear God who loveth us,
> He made and loveth all.[21]

They are lines, one might think, more likely to fall from the pious pen and socially conservative lips of Mrs. Cecil Frances Alexander, whose *Hymns for Little Children* (1848) are best remembered today for the words of 'All things bright and beautiful'. But here they are spoken by the ghostly, fearful 'grey-beard loon' of a Mariner, and written by the pen of Coleridge. They certainly do not seem to console or comfort the Wedding Guest, who departs 'like one that hath been stunned', a sadder and a wiser man. But wiser in what sense? Surely not, we might suppose, that he has learnt the simple lesson of Christian love for creation from the sinister Mariner? There is too much moral sentiment in that. The pure imagination leaves us more confused, or at least, very much less certain.

When Coleridge, the ironist, suggests that there is too much moral in 'The Rime of the Ancient Mariner' he is, I think, warning us against taking it too literally. Literalism was something against which he continually waged war. In *The Statesman's Manual* he wrote that 'A hunger-bitten and idea-less philosophy naturally produces a starveling and comfortless religion. It is among the miseries of the present age that it recognizes no medium between *Literal* and *Metaphorical*.'[22] The trite religion of the Mariner's last words is precisely intended to sound hollow, an 'obtrusion of the moral sentiment'. The Mariner is, after all, another version of the figure of Ahasuerus, as Immanuel Kant

---

21 'The Rime of the Ancient Mariner', *Poetical Works*, p. 209.
22 *Lay Sermons*, p. 30.

names the Wandering Jew, or the Flying Dutchman, doomed forever to wander the seas without rest or respite. Coleridge hated trite religious sentiments – precisely those of the kind we find in Mrs Barbauld's own poetry and prose with its simple doctrine of moral cause and effect, and entirely devoid of any imagination or irony. I cannot leave her without giving an example of her crass simplicity, her lack of imagination, which Coleridge would rightly regard as both utterly silly and highly dangerous:

> A naughty boy will not feed a starving and freezing robin; in fact he even pulls the poor bird's tail! It dies. Shortly after that, the boy's parents leave him because he is cruel, and he is forced to beg for food. He goes into a forest, sits down and cries, and is never heard of again; it is believed that bears ate him.[23]

Exit pursued by a bear.

Coleridge was utterly fascinated by the faculty of the imagination on which he wrote throughout his life, and nowhere more famously or concisely as in his *Biographia Literaria*. It is worth returning to once again:

> The primary IMAGINATION I hold to be the living Power and prime Agent of all human Perception, and as a repetition in the finite mind of the eternal act of creation in the infinite I AM. The secondary I consider as an echo of the former, co-existing with the conscious will, yet still as identical with the primary in the kind of its operation. It dissolves, diffuses, dissipates, in order to re-create; or where this process is rendered impossible, yet still at events it struggles to idealize and to unify. It is essentially *vital*, even as all objects (*as* objects) are essentially fixed and dead.[24]

In both his prose and in his verse you can almost hear and feel Coleridge thinking, and then thinking about thinking. Every thought and every word is weighed, qualified and considered and he demands a great deal of his reader. In the imagination, as in words themselves, his repeated insistence is upon its living quality, its open ended vitality, and

---

23 Mrs Barbauld, quoted in John Spencer Hill, *A Coleridge Companion* (London: Macmillan, 1983), p. 164.

24 *Biographia Literaria*, Vol. 1, p. 304.

this for him lies at the very heart of the poetic impulse. Poetry is not just about life; it is living, and alive with something very close to what in Christian theology, after the opening of St John's Gospel, is known as the 'logos' or vital divine Word. Coleridge even planned a lengthy work to be entitled the *Logosophia*, to which the *Biographia Literaria* was to be the introduction, though this *Logosophia* was never written: another prevarication. But it was to have been his definite statement against all mechanistic conceptions, a comprehensive expression of his sense of 'the One Life' in all things, as first visited in his early conversation poems, of which 'Frost at Midnight' is the purest.[25]

In his poetic imagination, a faculty of enormous intelligence, Coleridge travelled to realms hardly known to common humanity, places that are at once both dark as Erebus and yet suffused with a divine light that illuminates the very soul. It is sometimes said that after about 1810, Coleridge stopped writing poetry and that he had lost what, in the 'Dejection Ode' of 1802 he had called 'my shaping spirit of Imagination'. I do not think that this is the case, though a reader must be intrepid and must burrow deep to follow the thought and words of the older Coleridge, often with much of the puzzlement of those young men who listened to him on Highgate Hill in his old age – a sublime man, a king of men, incomprehensible, but somehow rather wonderful. In his later writings and notebooks, written privately and only partly, one feels, for the prying reader, Coleridge seems to speak somewhere between prose and verse, and in a form which approaches the language of prayer itself, though not actually addressed to God.

In a remarkable poem of 1817 entitled 'Limbo' he seems to be describing himself as an old man inhabiting a nether world, a limbo, and yet entranced like no-one since St Augustine himself, with the divine beauty at which he gazes, though blind, and his gaze is returned: he looks, inwardly as it were, into the eyes of God:

> 'Tis a strange place, this Limbo! – not a Place,
> Yet name it so; - where Time and weary Space
> Fettered from flight, with night-mare sense of fleeing,
> Strive for their last crepuscular half-being; -
> Lank Space, and scytheless Time with branny hands
> Barren and soundless as the measureless sands,

25 See further, Richard Holmes, *Coleridge: Darker Reflections* (London: HarperCollins, 1998), pp. 72-3.

Not mark'd by flit of Shades, - unmeaning they
As moonlight on the dial of the day!
But that is lovely – looks like Human Time,
An Old Man with a steady look sublime,
That stops his earthly task to watch the skies;
But he is blind – a Statue hath such eyes; -
Yet having moonward turn's his face by chance,
Gazes the orb with moon-like countenance,
With scant white hairs, with foretop bald and high,
He gazes still, - his eyeless face all eye; -
As 'twere an organ full of silent sight,
He whole face seemeth to rejoice in light!
Lip touching lip, all moveless, bust and limb –
He seems to gaze at that which seems to gaze on him![26]

The poem is perfect, so that nothing can be taken out of it. The blind 'Old Man' exists in a limbo beyond the limits of time and space, a place of disintegration and without shadows, provoking the impossible image of moonlight shining on a sundial. It is but an image of temporal reversal, later in the century to be joked about by Lewis Carroll in his comic poem 'The Walrus and the Carpenter', but in Coleridge the imagination draws us back, enthralled. The moon shines on the face of the sundial, and it *looks like* human time, even in this timeless limbo. The Old Man sees with his inward gaze, with the eye of the imagination, and that is enough. The image grows in power and strength – 'his eyeless face all eye'. In age Coleridge is returning to the divine poetry of 'Kubla Khan', but now a different figure, no longer dangerous but purely visionary. Faculties are merged in the 'silent sight' of his imagination until we reach a point of stillness and ecstasy worthy of a Meister Eckhart or a St John of the Cross.

The poem does continue beyond the lines that I have quoted, returning us to the darkness and non-being of limbo, a 'blank Naught-at-all' and 'positive Negation!'[27] But the blind poet, by the power of the imagination, can transcend even this utter negation, if only seemingly so. Coleridge, the worldly failure, can see beyond the walls of hell. His later notebooks, only fairly recently made available to the public, are full of writings of this kind, lodged somewhere between philosophical musings, poetry and prayer. In his final years the contradictions of

---

26 'Limbo', *Poetical Works*, p. 430.
27 Ibid., p. 431.

Coleridge's character and person became exaggerated, and no-one in English literature, except perhaps the half-mad William Blake, knew more of heaven and hell, and of both at the same time. The painter John Martin's great and hugely popular canvasses of heaven and judgement were not more precise, though certainly more immediately and popularly accessible.[28] No-one has ever caught the figure of the ageing, shambolic Coleridge so well as Carlyle in his *Life of Sterling*. We have already seen him surrounded by the bemused rising spirits of the young generation. Now we see him alone:

> The good man, he was now getting old, towards sixty perhaps; and gave you an idea of a life that had been full of sufferings; a life heavy-laden, half-vanquished, still swimming painfully in seas of manifold physical and other bewilderment.... The deep eyes of a light hazel, were as full of sorrow as of inspiration; confused pain looked mildly from them, as in a kind of mild astonishment . . . expressive of weakness under possibility of strength.[29]

I have suggested that Coleridge was not the greatest of English poets. In a way, perhaps he simply *thought* too much. For a true poet is neither a philosopher nor a theologian, but inspired by and sometimes beyond both. And the poet's freedoms are different from those of either philosopher or theologian. Coleridge was a deeply poetic and religious *thinker*, who had moments – and as is often the case they were sometimes moments of weakness or despair – of profound poetry in his pen. His religious 'position' in later life is very difficult to define, for in a certain way he came back to the Church of England of his childhood and for the ministry of which his clerical father had once destined him, but never entirely or simply so. There was always something of the pantheist in Coleridge, seeing God in all things, and the sense of a divine unity in creation perceived in the life of words, those 'living educts of the imagination' and in the interweaving of images often in profound contradictions. You can be in heaven and hell at the same moment, and in a moment that is also outside time. Perhaps his closest

---

28 John Martin's (1789-1854) great paintings of biblical scenes, of heaven and of hell, brought him enormous fame at the same time as Coleridge was writing poems like 'Limbo'. Martin's first popular success was *Joshua Commanding the Sun to Stand Still* (1816), painted in the year before the poem was written.

29 Thomas Carlyle, *Selected Writings*, p. 316.

poetical companion in the nineteenth century, though divided by years and many circumstances, is the Jesuit Gerard Manley Hopkins, though his theological route via the theology of Duns Scotus was very different. But he too could see the divine in all created things and even in the swoop of a hawk, and yet also know the despair of the 'dead letter' in the Terrible Sonnets written in misery at the end of his life in Ireland.

Coleridge's religious and theological influence on the nineteenth century was broad, deep, and it is extremely hard to pin down. His late book *On the Constitution of Church and State According to the Idea of Each* (1830) has been described as 'the only one of his works which achieved anything like a popular success',[30] and it is certainly something of a classic of conservative thought in English. But I doubt if it was half as influential (not least in the United States of America) as the mazy, unsystematic musings and aphorisms contained in *Aids to Reflection* (1825), where Coleridge famously inveighs against the mechanics of 'evidences', insisting that in religion we must make people *feel* the want of it – we are back again to the living power of words. My favourite aphorism in *Aids to Reflection* is XXV:

> He, who begins by loving Christianity better than Truth, will proceed by loving his own Sect or Church better than Christianity, and end in loving himself better than all.[31]

If he had never written anything else we would remember Coleridge for this. Towards the close of his life Coleridge certainly went some way to being reconciled with the Church of England and he is deeply theistic in all his thought and writings. He never finally left God, nor, I think, did God leave him. But above all Coleridge is devoted to the pursuit of truth as that which binds together the living and dynamic unity of all creation. It is a teaching we might well remember today in our time of dangerous 'post-truth'.

It is to Coleridge that we owe the idea of the 'clerisy' – that notion of a secular intellectual élite in the country that was capable of understanding and sustaining the best in a national culture, largely through the presence in each parish community of an educated person – usually the parson – who represented the best in society on the basis

---

30 Basil Willey, *Samuel Taylor Coleridge* (London: Chatto and Windus, 1972), p. 236, quoting J. Colmer.

31 S.T. Coleridge, *Aids to Reflection* [1825] (London: G. Bell and Sons, 1913), p. 66.

of the principles of godliness and good learning. In our own time when any form of intellectualism is under huge pressure, such a proposal may attract criticism, though perhaps it behoves us to re-think Coleridge's vision for our own time. And despite his dislike of the Toad of Priesthood (and Coleridge was often lacking in consistency), he was from the time of the *Biographia Literaria* (1817) convinced of the crucial role of the national church in the well-being of the nation. In *Biographia* he wrote that, 'still the church presents to every man of learning and genius a profession, in which he may cherish a rational hope of being able to unite the widest schemes of literary utility with the strictest performance of professional duties'.[32] This may seem very far from our present culture and even further, sadly, from our contemporary, increasingly business-like Church of England. But it remains with us as a *vision* – and perhaps a poetic vision. And it is deeply rooted in Coleridge's intense intelligence – *Biographia Literaria* is an exercise in reflecting on how we read and come to understand, not least by irony and indirectness. It is all about thinking. This vision is also rooted in his deep sense of religion and sacramentalism, though he would probably have called it a matter of symbol rather than sacrament. In another glowing sentence from *The Statesman's Manual*, Coleridge wrote:

> a Symbol . . . is characterized by a translucence of Special in the Individual or of the General in the Especial or of the Universal in the General. Above all by a translucence of the Eternal through and in the Temporal. It always partakes of the Reality which it render intelligible; and while it enunciates the whole, abides itself as a living part in that Unity, of which it is the representative.[33]

This is written with typical precision and balance. It is also deeply poetic in Coleridge's terms, demanding that response of faith that requires both the willing and the intelligent suspension of disbelief. Such faith is not an abandonment of the intellectual faculty but requires rather its most careful application so that the act of faith in the suspension of disbelief, is something considered and intelligent. It is clear how this becomes a beginning for John Henry Newman's careful assessment of the nature of the assent of faith and belief in his great work *A Grammar of Assent* (1870).

---

32 *Biographia Literaria*, Vol. 1, p. 226.
33 *Lay Sermons*, p. 30.

I do not regret having spent so much of my life thinking, or trying to think, about Samuel Taylor Coleridge, and of my books, I think that the first, with its rather plodding title, *Coleridge as Poet and Religious Thinker*, remains my favourite, though it is now largely forgotten and a little dated. It was written, after all, many years ago and it is, of course, very very far from perfect. But then one may recall that another commentator on Coleridge in his Highgate Hill days was the essayist Charles Lamb, who wrote to William Wordsworth on 26 August, 1816, referring to Coleridge's addiction to laudanum:

> I think his essentials not touched: he is very bad, but then he wonderfully picks up another day, and his face when he repeats his verses hath its ancient glory, an Archangel a little damaged.[34]

And among these verses of this damaged Archangel there is 'Kubla Khan', one of the most glorious, mysterious images in English poetry, and the closest, perhaps, to that sense of divine creation in the poet that was God's from the beginning. With such poetry we may return for a moment to the original perfection of Paradise, before it all went wrong. Or, at least we may glimpse it. Is Coleridge just mad, soaked in drugs or touched with the sublime for that one moment: an Archangel a little damaged?

> For he on honeydew hath fed,
> And drunk the milk of Paradise.

Now we turn back yet further, to the seventeenth century and a very different poet in the Anglican tradition – Thomas Traherne.

---

34 Frontispiece to Norman Fruman, *Coleridge: The Damaged Archangel* (London: George Allen & Unwin, 1971).

Thomas Traherne
(1636-1674)

4.
Thomas Traherne:
Objects of Happiness

The fourth chapter of this book takes us into a very different, more ancient, world from that of either Thomas Hardy or Samuel Taylor Coleridge. We think also about a poet whose acquaintance I made relatively recently, but whom I have quickly grown to love and respect, not least as I have been tutored in the reading of poetry by Coleridge. One thing leads to another. From the confusions of nineteenth century faith and doubt – the age of the critical spirit and the will to believe - we go back to the late Renaissance world of the seventeenth century, a time in English life and literature in which religion and Christian theology were the inescapable, driving forces that shaped the world of all people. Among the disparate group of seventeenth century poets that were first described by Dr Samuel Johnson as the 'metaphysicals',[1] the best known to us are George Herbert and John Donne, both Anglican clergymen and both acknowledged as major poets. But I want to focus on a different figure – the far less well-known Thomas Traherne (1637-74), also an Anglican clergyman and parish priest, having, as well, in common with Herbert the fact that he died young,

---

1   Johnson's reference to the metaphysical poets in his 'Life of Cowley' written in1777, was dismissive and disparaging in the extreme. *The Lives of the Poets* [1779-81] 2 Vols. (Oxford: Oxford University Press, 1968), Vol. 1, p. 13.

in his thirties. Indeed, until recently so little regarded was Traherne that Helen Gardner in her old but still standard anthology of *The Metaphysical Poets* (1975) prints only two of his poems (as opposed to forty two by Donne), describing him as a 'forgotten Restoration divine',[2] while T.S. Eliot's oft reprinted essay 'The Metaphysical Poets' (1921) does not mention Traherne even once.

None of Traherne's poems and only one prose work, the anti-Catholic *Roman Forgeries* (1673) were published in his lifetime. He prepared a work entitled *Christian Ethicks* for press but then died in the year before it was published in 1675. Until recently he was regarded as what university courses in literature, after Eliot, like to describe as a 'minor poet', but by a rather remarkable, indeed almost miraculous, series of events the bulk of his writings in poetry and prose have only recently come to light and now are being made available to the public. Traherne's modern recovery began when William Brooke, an amateur bibliophile, bought a notebook containing poems and prose for a few pence from a London bookstall in the winter of 1896-7, and these were subsequently identified by the scholar Bertram Dobell as being by Traherne. Dobell published them as the *Poetical Works* (1903) and the *Centuries of Meditations* (1908). Only now is a splendid collected edition of Traherne's writings becoming available under the editorship of Jan Ross. Six substantial volumes are currently available of a projected nine-volume set, due to be completed in 2020. Most bizarrely, the leather-bound manuscript of the unfinished work known as *Commentaries of Heaven*, written 'For the Satisfaction of Atheists, & the Consolation of Christians', was rescued from a burning rubbish heap, the covers already alight, by a Mr and Mrs Wookey of Lancashire in the 1960s. It travelled with them to Canada when they emigrated there, and was not identified as an original writing of Traherne until 1981, some of the pins attaching the paper to the binding being original from the seventeenth century. Even more recently, some of Traherne's works were discovered by Julia Smith and Laetitia Yeandle in the Folger Library in Washington DC, and by a Cambridge scholar, Jeremy Maule, in 1997 in Lambeth Palace Library, London, again quite by accident. It seems quite possible that there are more writings still to come to light from references to yet unknown poems and prose works in the works that we now have. Readers today

---

2   Helen Gardner, *The Metaphyscal Poets*. (Harmondsworth: Penguin, 1972), p. 321.

also have the benefit of some outstanding critical books on Traherne that reveal him not only as a fine poet but a faithful parish priest and a significant theologian and thinker, an obsessive reader who was learned, among other things, in the early Church Fathers, seventeenth century theology and the scientific discussions and debates of his time. Especially important for me has been the work of the late Denise Inge in her book *Wanting Like a God* (2009), and Elizabeth S. Dodd and her book *Boundless Innocence in Thomas Traherne's Poetic Theology* (2015).

The point of saying all this is so that you can see that my love affair with Traherne's work was very different from my boyhood obsession with Hardy. It is very recent and differently acquired, and therefore rather distinct, much more academic and theological, and perhaps, I readily admit a bit more laboured. I still do not feel quite as comfortable with Traherne as with my older loves.

Thomas Traherne, as we shall see, was not only an Oxford-trained theologian but much more he *saw* the world theologically: and in the seventeenth century this did not exclude also seeing it with the reasoned eye of what was then understood as science. It was not until the nineteenth century that religion and science went their seemingly separate ways, very largely after the publication of Charles Darwin's *Origin of Species* in 1859. For Traherne the vision of Christian theology as part of a rational perspective on all reality in one complex unity embraced and upheld his whole understanding and vision. If Hardy saw the world as an outsider to religion, Traherne in a different age, saw it very much from the inside out. He could not have questioned this perspective and would have called it looking with the eyes of the soul. His first modern literary editor, the Victorian amateur book-lover William Brooke – the man who discovered the work that we now know as the *Centuries of Meditations* together with some poems in 1896 – mistook Traherne's work for that of his contemporary poet, and close neighbour, the Welsh medical doctor Henry Vaughan, and it is easy to see why. Both of them have an extraordinary poetic capacity to see the world at once in both its everyday aspect and in the context of divinity. Vaughan's most famous poem begins with the line, 'I saw eternity the other night'.[3] It is almost off-hand, a throw-away line, as if this were a perfectly common occurrence; and for both Vaughan and

---

3   Henry Vaughan, *Poetry and Selected Prose*, ed. by L.C. Martin (Oxford: Oxford University Press, 1963), p. 299.

Traherne, in a way, it was. That was how they experienced the world
and eternity, all at once. I will have a little bit more to say about time
and eternity later on.

But first a word about Traherne himself, though actually we know
very little of the details of his life. He was born in 1636, and spent most
of his life in and around the cathedral city of Hereford. He seems to
have been born into a reasonably flourishing family that can best be
described as part of the new rising middle class, with enough money to
send him as a student to Brasenose College, Oxford. Ordained in 1660,
most of the remainder of his life was associated with the rural parish
of Credenhall in Herefordshire, where, it is recorded, 'he visited the
poor and instructed the youth',[4] – a faithful parish priest – and from
1669 he was also Chaplain to Sir Orlando Bridgeman, Lord Keeper
of the Seal. He was not, therefore, unaware of the wider world. He
died young in October 1674. Although an insistent theme of his poetry
is that of innocence, combined with a genuine wonder of the natural
world, Traherne was clearly a man of profound learning, knowing
both theology and the classics as well as Renaissance philosophy and
a great deal about contemporary scientific theory. He seems to have
been associated with the group of Anglican theologians known as
the Cambridge Platonists – thinkers of the distinction of Peter Sterry,
Ralph Cudworth and Henry More, whose thought was constituted
by an absorption of Platonic philosophy, rationalism, but also the
Christian mystical tradition. This connection is evident throughout
Traherne's work. He was clearly a man who set great store by reason,
but who also saw the world at different levels simultaneously, the
eternal in the temporal and the temporal in the eternal. (Coleridge,
who read deeply in the Cambridge Platonists, would have understood
this perfectly.)

Ideas in Traherne are rarely simple. Innocence for him is not a
childish virtue but is associated with wisdom and is something learnt
or perhaps recovered as a kind of 'second naïveté', that term which is
now so closely associated with the work of the French philosopher
Paul Ricoeur.[5] But at the heart of all Traherne's thinking and poetry is
the idea of 'felicitie', a joy known as, in the fine words of one critic, 'an

---

4   Quoted in Denise Inge, Introduction to *Thomas Traherne: Poetry and Prose*.
    (London: SPCK, 2002), p. xv.
5   See further Paul Ricoeur, *The Symbolism of Evil*. Trans. Emerson Buchanan
    (Boston: Beacon Press, 1969), and above, p. 22.

intense and learned activity [of] conceptual thought working on living memory'.[6] Traherne's unfinished, encyclopedic work *Commentaries of Heaven* is described on its first page as a book:

WHEREIN
The Mysteries of Felicitie
are opened
and
ALL THINGS
Discovered
to be
Objects of Happiness.[7]

Being here at the very heart of Traherne's thinking and poetry, now let us turn to his writings themselves – in both prose and verse, though it is sometimes difficult to distinguish the difference in him. He sees with a poet's eye, with a kind of intuitive insight that does not forsake learning,[8] and he clearly appreciates life to the full both in body, mind and soul. Almost all of Traherne's writings stand somewhere between prayer and statement, the public and the private. Here is a passage from early in the *Centuries of Meditations*, on the proper enjoyment of wine:

Wine by its Moysture quencheth my Thirst, whether I consider it or no: but to see it flowing from his Lov who gav it unto Man, Quencheth the Thirst even of the Holy Angels. To consider it, is to Drink it Spritualy. To rejoice in its Diffusion is to be of a Publick Mind. And to take Pleasure in all the Benefits it doth to all is Heavenly: for so they do in Heaven. To do so, is to be Divine and Good: and to imitate our Infinit and Eternal Father.[9]

---

6   Francis King, 'Thomas Traherne: Intellect and Felicity' (1972), quoted in Denise Inge, *Wanting Like a God: Desire and Freedom in Thomas Traherne* (London: SCM, 2009), p. 23.

7   *The Works of Thomas Traherne*. Vol. II, ed. by Jan Ross (Cambridge: Brewer, 2007), p. 3

8   See, Cassandra Gorman, 'Thomas Traherne's Intuitive Knowledge of "ALL THINGS" in the Commentaries of Heaven', ed. by Ineke Bockting, Jennifore Kilgore-Caradec and Cathy Parcs. *Poetry and Religion: Figures of the Sacred* (Bern: Peter Lang, 2013), pp. 35-53.

9   *Centuries of Meditations*, 'The First Century', 27, quoted in Denise Inge, *Thomas Traherne: Poetry and Prose*, pp. 3-4. (Henceforth, *TTPP*).

Traherne moves easily between worlds, and seems to live comfortably and at the same time in both his soul and his body. You can see why he read the Song of Songs so well:[10] and he liked his glass of wine, in moderation, a pleasure he shared with the angels themselves.

The *Centuries* move on to the theme of enjoying the world aright – 'felicitie' – and here he begins to turn language to his own purposes, or perhaps to purge it of the taint of sin. The commandments warn us against covetousness – but Traherne borrows the word and turns it around in a moment, we might almost say, of linguistic salvation. He writes that, 'You never Enjoy the World aright, til you so lov the Beauty of Enjoying it, that you are Covetous and Earnest to Persuade others to Enjoy it.'[11] And if the happiest are those who need nothing, Traherne uses this idea (taken, he says, from Socrates) to embark upon a remarkable passage on the Wants of God. Again, he seeks to purge the very word itself, 'want' being an impatient and often petulant term in our vocabulary, but now changed for our better use, suspended between the older sense of want as 'lack' and the more modern sense of 'desire'.[12] Traherne begins: 'This is very strange that GOD should Want: for in Him is the Fulness of all Blessedness.' But there is, of course, more than one meaning to this word in his hands. Traherne is a true metaphysical for whom words burst with different levels of meaning. Can God be either desirous of anything or in want, that is, in *need*? God, after all, can want for nothing.

I wonder here if Traherne was thinking of the first verse of Psalm 23 in the King James Version: 'The Lord is my shepherd, I shall not want'. For now comes the turning point:

> But [God] Wanted Angels and Men, Images, Companions. And these He had from all Eternitie.
>
> (43) Infinit Wants Satisfied Produce infinit Joys; And, in the Possession of those Joys, are infinit Joys themselves. *The Desire Satisfied is a Tree of Life* . . . GOD was never without this Tree of Life. He did Desire infinitly.[13]

10 'Old Testament quotations throughout Traherne's *Kingdom of God* draw particularly on the Psalms, Proverbs and Song of Songs'. Elizabeth S. Dodd, *Boundless Innocence in Thomas Traherne's Poetic Theology* (Farnham: Ashgate, 2015), p. 155.

11 *TTPP*, p. 3.

12 See, Inge, *Wanting Like a God*, pp. 29-31.

13 *TTPP*, from *Centuries of Meditations*, 'The First Century', 42-3, p. 6.

It is a remarkable piece of poetic reasoning, whereby our human 'wants', in God's created world, become 'sacred Occasions and Means of Felicitie'. This last word is, as we have seen, one of Traherne's favourites, reminding us again that he is a true metaphysical poet, endlessly playing with the riches of language. As in the poetry of John Donne, he can use shocking terms – we may be ravished by God's love for us, for example – but as words spin and turn, purified in the alchemy of his usage, they finally come to rest in the great terms – Traherne might call them principles – like 'felicitie', 'love', 'beauty', 'freedom', 'innocence'. He was, after all, a Platonist.

And so he concludes his treatise on 'want'. He is quite clear and bold: 'You must Want like a GOD, that you may be Satisfied like GOD. Were you not made in His *Image*?' And then there is a gentle, moderate warning, to '*be Sensible of your Wants, that you may be sensible of your Treasures*.'[14] Again – our model is God himself, for God is sensible of all things, a passionate God who loves and desires. The very words that express our fallen, needy and *wanting* condition are being taken into God – and we are thereby transformed, or perhaps better expressed as transfigured.

One hundred and fifty years before William Wordsworth celebrated the wisdom of the child in the poems of the *Lyrical Ballads*, Traherne's *Centuries*, anticipating the Romantic vision of childhood, present us with a remarkable moment of childlike 'reason'. He writes, perhaps, one may think, a little precociously:

> Once I remember (I think I was about 4 yeer old, when) I thus reasoned with my self; sitting in a little Obscure Room in my Fathers poor House. If there be a God, certainly He must be infinit in Goodness. And that I was prompted to, by a real Whispering Instinct of Nature.[15]

Traherne, it seems, was a very bright youngster. But like the Romantics William Blake, Coleridge and Wordsworth after him, he is fascinated by the child's view of things. Yet for him this instinctive wisdom is not so much of nature as of a divine origin, its roots in the teachings of Jesus in the gospels. And for us as adults it is something that can be learnt again. In a poem entitled 'The Salutation' he imagines the innocent wonder of the child as it emerges into the world after thousands upon thousands of years of lying beneath the dust 'in

---

14 Ibid., 44-5, p. 7.
15 *TTPP*, 'The Third Century', 16, p. 23.

a Chaos'. Each and every birth of a child is a new creation. (I should remark here that Traherne, like most people of his time, thought that the world was, give or take, about 5,000 years old. It makes sense in a way: go seventeen hundred years back to Christ, two thousand more takes us back to Abraham, add another thousand or so and you are back to Adam and Eve and the beginning: about 5,000 altogether. Archbishop Ussher [1581-1656] was famously much more precise, setting the creation as being on 23 October, 4004 BC). In the newly created innocence of the child the soul, our humanity's purest part, shines most clearly. Traherne regards human beings as made up of body and soul, one yet also clearly two, the body becoming weighed down with 'dross and matter' as we grow older. He would find this idea everywhere in the writings of the Cambridge Platonists. But sin never finally overwhelms us. Traherne, on the latitudinarian edges of Protestant orthodoxy, is far more deeply aware of the glory that is in the soul of each one of us, finally overwhelming sin and shining most brightly in the innocence of childhood as the child's eyes are first opened on the world created by God:

> Long time before
> I in my Mother Womb was born,
> A GOD preparing did this Glorious Store,
>   The World for me adorne.
> Into this Eden so Divine and fair,
> So Wide and Bright, I com his Son and Heir.
>
> A Stranger here
> Strange Things doth meet, Strange Glories See;
> Strange Treasures lodg'd in the fair World appear,
>   Strange all, and New to me.
> But that they mine should be, who nothing was,
> That Strangest is of all, yet brought to pass.[16]

We have here also an example of what theology calls *theosis*. Traherne found it in the Hermetic tradition of the *Corpus Hermeticum* and the writings of the great Renaissance teachers Marsilio Ficino (1433-99) and Giovanni Pico della Mirandola (1463-94), though it can also be traced back to very early Christian teaching. Quite simply put, *theosis* is the recognition that humanity stands between the temporal and

---

16 'The Salutation', from the Dobell Manuscript, *TTPP*, p. 39.

the eternal realms, drawn into divinity by God in Christ, for, as St Athanasius wrote in the fourth century in his work *De Incarnatione*, God 'was made man in order that we might be made God'.

We have a long theological essay by Traherne delightfully entitled *A Sober View of Dr Twisses his Considerations*, in which he engages with one of the most bitterly fought religious debates of his time, the Calvinist/Arminian division about the question of free will. For the strict Calvinist our human nature is mired in sin and unable to achieve anything without the grace of God. We are bound to our sinful nature. For the Arminians, however, and for Traherne, bordering on the ancient heresy called Pelagianism that St Augustine had fought in the fourth century, human nature is created by God and therefore must be fundamentally good and able, despite the accumulations of sin, to exercise free will and realise, of itself, the beauty and joy of all creation. In the child the precious soul shines most clearly and the child sees the world with the eyes of the soul. Later, more secularly inclined poets might have called this the faculty of the imagination. You see how things come together in poetry. For Traherne, as children we are born into an 'Eden so Divine and fair' – the world as it was before the Fall and paradise regained. The child comes to the world as a stranger, viewing, with perhaps a faint echo of Prospero's Miranda, its strange new wonders. The child is nothing and still is given all things in perception. Yet Traherne's sense of innocence is neither sentimental nor soft. It is something that in us may be learnt, or perhaps re-learnt, as he builds, in the words of Elizabeth Dodd, 'on a tradition of interpretation that identifies innocence as an aspect of holiness, associated with harmlessness, guiltlessness, sinlessness, simplicity and trust.'[17]

In another poem, Traherne describes the soul as a 'naked, simple life' and the essence of being, and here he is at his most 'metaphysical', teasing the words into meaning and using mathematical puzzles just as elsewhere he plays with time and relativity. He plays with the idea, the optical illusion, that as we move past objects they seem to move and we therefore seem to stand still. He speaks of the innocent soul as it perceives the world:

> It Acts not from a Centre to
>   Its Object as remote,
> But present is, when it doth view,

---

17 Elizabeth S. Dodd, op. cit. p. 1.

Being with the Being it doth note.
    Whatever it doth do,
It doth not by another Engine work,
But by it self; which in the Act doth lurk.
Its Essence is Transformed into a true
    And perfect Act.[18]

Traherne is thinking precisely here like a scientist, observing how things work and act in relation to one another. The soul is the very centre of all things, but in its working – its action – it is never remote, as the centre from the periphery, but absolutely present to that which it sees. It never works by proxy, but works essentially; its essence is in all action and perception. In short, the innocent soul is perfectly one with all things, just as we, in our fallen adulthood, are distanced and remote, struggling in our blighted perceptions.

And yet in one extraordinary exercise of the poetic imagination taken from a work entitled *The Kingdom of God* that explores the beauty of the created earth, Traherne suggests what the earth may seem like to a wondering 'celestial stranger' who has lived, hitherto 'at vast and prodigious Distances from the Earth'. What does the earth seem like to a being from another world or planet? Wonderment is unbounded and for page after page Traherne celebrates life on earth with a joy that we might find hard to follow in our age of pollution, environmental destruction and dramatic climate change. Here are just three short examples of his great, extraordinary litany to beauty:

1. Such Lions & Leopards, & fourefooted Beasts; such innumerable Companies, & Hosts of Insects; such an Ocean of fishes, Whales & Syrens, surprizing him in the Sea; such Kidneys of Wheat in the fat & abundant Valleys; such Quarries of Stones, & so Many Mines & Mettals in the Hills.

2. Such Combinations of States, & Common Wealths; such Kingdoms & Ages; such Bookes & Universities; such Colleges & Libraries; such Trades & Studies; such Occupations & Professions; such Retirements & Devotions; such Altars & Temples; such Holy Days, & Sabbaths; such vows & prayers.

18 'My Spirit', *TTPP*, p. 2.

3. [Of children] They are conceived with Pleasure, & come forth of the Womb to Innumerable Blessings; They are dandled in their Infancy upon the knees of Ladies, & are the Delights of their parents; Their Fathers and Mothers minister unto them, they are embraced with kisses, & satisfied with Loves; They drink Honey & Nectar from their Lips in Childhood, and grow up to greater enjoyments.[19]

If Traherne portrays an ideal world, it is even more wonderful how he can find a pre-lapsarian perfection, the perfect Paradise of an unfallen world, in the very stuff of our everyday life – perceiving beauty in things as miscellaneous as quarries, college libraries and trades, as well as the nurturing of children. And he is never coy, as in celebrating the spiritual perfections of the soul, neither does he belittle with puritan disapproval the joys of sex, noting approvingly that children are 'conceived with Pleasure'.

In an even more extraordinary celebration of the beauty of all creation, Traherne takes the most unpromising of subjects, the common blow-fly, and succeeds in making this, to us, the most annoying of insects truly magnificent, alongside woodlice, spiders, beetles and dormice. It is as if he tried to think of the most unprepossessing creatures in all creation and then realise them as magnificent creatures of God, out of the sheer joy of all creation. Here is Traherne describing the blow-fly:

The Creation of Insects affords us a Clear Mirror of Almighty Power, and Infinit Wisdom with a prospect likewise of Transcendent Goodness. Had but one of those curious and High stomached Flies, been created, whose Burnisht, & Resplendent Bodies are like Orient Gold, or Polisht Steel; whose Wings are so strong, & whose Head so crowned with an Imperial Tuff . . . doubtless he would hav been amazed at the Height of His estate.

Traherne goes on to describe the fly and its actions in the minutest of detail, a whole world unto itself:

The exact & curious Symmetry of all his parts, the feeling of his feet, & the swiftness of his Wings, the vivacity of his Quick & Active Power, the vigor of his Resentments, his Passions, &

---

19 *The Kingdom of God*, from the Lambeth Manuscript, *TTPP*, pp. 112-13.

Affections . . . would make him seem a Treasure wherein all
Wonders were shut up together, & that God had done as much
in little there, as he had done at large in the whole World. [20]

I especially like in this description of the fly 'the vigor of his resentments'.
Think of Traherne the next time a fly relentlessly keeps on returning to
the food placed on the table however many times it is swatted away –
and be thankful for God's work in creation!

Traherne was writing long before his fellow poet William Blake
invited us, more famously, to see the world in a grain of sand, and in
some ways his conceit of the fly is even more wonderful and instructive
of the unitary and cohesive power of the imagination. He teaches us
felicitie even in things that we find at best tiresome. Traherne finally
suggests that if nothing else living on earth existed except this one fly,
then God's power, wisdom and goodness would be evident, and to
illustrate this truth of creation he uses this most despised and disliked
of creaturely irritants. Blake, on the other hand, when contemplating
the mystery of creation, had to have recourse to the magnificence of
the tiger in all its majesty. But Traherne contemplates the mystery and
wonder of all things – in a common blow-fly.

Thomas Traherne wrote poems on leaping over the moon,
contemplating reflections in the water beneath our feet, and seeing
ever-new worlds in the world around us. Some of his poems in the
sequence known as *Thanksgivings*, published as *A Serious and Pathetical
Contemplation* in 1699, merge into prayers that draw on the Psalms
or the familiar canticles of the Anglican *Book of Common Prayer*. In
one of my favourites, entitled 'Thanksgivings for the Soul', his almost
mathematical appreciation of the wonders of creation finally breaks
into the familiar words of the *Benedicite* (as Thomas Hardy's *Tess of
the D'Urbervilles* does also, Tess bursting into a song of thanksgiving,
even after her tragedy, when she descends into the natural beauties of
the Valley of the Great Dairies, finding regeneration and new life in
the wonder of creation): 'O ye Powers of mine immortal Soul, bless
ye the Lord, praise him, and magnifie him for ever'.[21] Like his fellow
metaphysical poet, the Revd George Herbert, Traherne is saturated in
the language and phrases of the *Book of Common Prayer* and the King
James Bible, both of which he would have read daily as a priest in the

---

20 Ibid., pp. 111-12.
21 'Thanksgivings for the Soul', from the *Thanksgivings*, *TTPP*, p. 58.

morning and evening offices of the church, and they inform his poetry just as his poetry brings them to new life. St Paul's great hymn to love in I Corinthians 13 lies behind the five qualities of the 'Soul within':

Spiritual
Heavenly
Divine
Intelligent
Profitable

Beside these qualities he writes: 'That doth not fill, but feeleth all Things. Receiveth. Seeth, discerneth, enjoyeth them'. [22] Traherne's Christian vision never dissociates thinking from feeling or joy. They stand together.

If Thomas Hardy's poetry exists utterly outside the theological realm, prompting a response that theology can barely rise to, then Traherne's verse is thoroughly inside a theological, Christian utterance that realises the world that God has created in all its theological magnificence. It is a vision that makes Traherne so difficult and so tantalizing for the religiously bereft and theologically under-educated modern reader. And, to add to the difficulty, one of his most tantalizing poems drawing on biblical inspiration is unfinished, though still of a formidable one thousand eight hundred lines. It is called 'The Ceremonial Law' and describes the descent of Moses from Mount Sinai, a vision at once too glorious to be looked upon, and yet one that draws every gaze to it. As one of Traherne's best modern readers, Denise Inge has so beautifully described his Moses: 'Himself untouched, he seems untouchable while all he touches is transformed and all they cannot touch allures'.[23] But gradually the light in the face of Moses that 'ravished' the people, its brightness far beyond their endurance, becomes something gentler – 'At last the Terror turns into a Smile' – and Moses becomes the human teacher of the unendurable divine truths that he has brought from the mountain. The 'man of flame' before whom the people fled, has become the humble teacher:

But Moses knew not that his face did Shine,
He that is humble he is most Divine. . ..

For then in truth we only are divine,
When Wisdom Love & Goodness in us shine,

---

22 'Thanksgivings for the Soul', *TTPP*, p. 59.
23 *TTPP*, p. 37.

And being full of Heavenly Blessedness
Ourselvs, make others with us to possess
The Glory we enjoy.[24]

Traherne's profound theology, indeed his considerable learning in early Christian thought, the Cambridge Platonists following Richard Hooker, and contemporary churchmen, bishops and poets like Lancelot Andrewes, Jeremy Taylor and George Herbert, often lies hidden. It is embedded in his verse and prose that capture for us, in the changes in Moses' face as he descends from Mount Sinai, the tone of awe, wonder and mystery experienced in the face of God. Gradually this becomes translated in Moses the teacher, to the essence of the religious life lived on earth. Truths too terrible to contemplate become the stuff of divinity here on earth, that which Herbert described in his poem 'Prayer (I)' as 'heaven in ordinary': for Traherne, Moses brings with him a Glory, and his teachings:

Gently strive
At least their putrid Coarses to revive
And fill their Tents with that Diviner Light
Which in the Mountain ravished our Sight.[25]

Note that little phrase, 'at least' – Traherne, for all his wonder at God's world, is a teacher who never expects too much. He would have understood the words of another, much later Christian poet, Cardinal Newman, 'One step enough for me'.

One of Traherne's most extensive works is entitled *Christian Ethicks*, published in the year after his death. For him the culmination of all ethics and Christian virtues is *gratitude* as the expression of the soul that has desired or felt want (a rich word that we have explored already) and has had desire fulfilled, as human need is met by divine plenitude. But if we begin with desire, what is its origin, and what is the nature of true desire, that which Traherne calls 'this soaring, sacred thirst'? Such proper desire is the very opposite of lust or greed, but rather the beginning of the love that is its motive. God's want or desire for us is met by our desire for God, and the soul that burns at its brightest in infancy, has an infinite capacity for love as the desire that leads to true felicity. In one poem Traherne praises God for the desire that was implanted in him from birth, a 'virgin

---

24 'The Ceremonial Law', *TTPP*, p. 65.
25 Ibid.

Infant Flame', or rather, an 'Inward Hidden Heavenly Love' that keeps him restless with a 'Heavenly Avarice' that is never satisfied.[26] Note again how Traherne employs the power of strong words and transfigures them for his own good, permitted use as we become avaricious for God.

The infant soul desires a 'paradise unknown' – a joy beyond our imagining. Then Traherne goes back, once again to the Bible, to the familiar figure of the suffering servant in Isaiah or the tortured figure of Psalm 22:

> Parched my Withered Bones
> And Eys did seem: My Soul was full of Groans.

The child grows into a fallen world, and yet all its sufferings and wounds arise from desire and love. The soul aches for the beloved, so that Traherne comes to a typically metaphysical paradox:

> O Happiness! A Famine burns,
> And all my Life to Anguish turns![27]

For this poet the miseries of life are born not so much of sin (more of that in a moment) but from the burning of desire to realise the paradise of heaven. For Traherne, they are the prelude to true 'felicitie'.

In the third stanza of this poem he writes of the false joys of 'Dead Material Toys' – that is 'Fruits, Flowers, Bowers, Shady Groves and Springs' – none of which add up to true 'Heavenly Joys'. These sylvan images are, of course, the stuff of Renaissance pastoral poetry since Edmund Spenser and Sir Philip Sidney in the previous century and before. But even as he dismisses them as dead material toys, Traherne also uses them to create an image of the Paradise that his soul desires, and in the next stanza they are again transfigured, turned upon the opening words – 'O Love!' The earthly paradise, that elsewhere he celebrates through the perception of the unsullied infant soul, and the joys of creation, are now transformed in what in poetics is known as an *epithalamium* – Spenser indeed wrote one of the most celebrated of these in English – that is a wedding poem, a poetic form that finds its origins in the biblical Song of Songs itself. The Alexandrian theologian Origen in the third century wrote a commentary on the Song in which he describes it as an *epithalamium*, 'a wedding song, written by Solomon

---

26 "Desire", *TTPP*, pp. 48-9.
27 Ibid., p. 49.

in the form of a play'.[28] Being a good Platonist, Thomas Traherne knows that the joys of earth replicate the perfect joys of heaven, when the human itself becomes transfigured into the divine:

> Ye Feasts and Living Pleasures!
> Ye Senses, Honors, and Imperial Treasures!
> Ye Bridal joys! Ye High Delights;
> That satisfy all Appetites!

In another context we might, perhaps, condemn Traherne as a sensualist (and indeed he is no prude in the matter of sexuality, though in him the erotic is truly celebrated in divine love).[29] But this is the Messianic Banquet, the Wedding Feast of the Lamb, and its joys must be fully savoured and entirely, wholly appropriated:

> Ye must, before I am Divine,
> In full Proprietie be mine.

Like John Donne, Traherne employs a daring range of vocabulary and image, and transforms, indeed transfigures them into the heavenly pleasures of divine desire and love. He feels to the full the joys of the material world and finds them perfected in heaven:

> These are the true and real Joys,
> The Living Flowing Inward Melting, Bright
> And Heavenly Pleasures; all the rest are Toys:
> All which are founded in Desire,
> As Light in Flame, and Heat in fire.[30]

In only one work, known to us as the *Select Meditations*, written when Traherne was in his twenties, does he spend much time on the subject of sin. Brought up under the influence of a Puritan education, at least until he went up as a student to Oxford, Traherne would have been expected to engage in careful self-scrutiny and reflections upon his unworthiness, yet his natural sense of the joy and beauty in creation is always more powerful and comes more readily to his pen. Thus he writes, in a language familiar to us drawn from Psalm 51 in the King James Bible:

---

28 Origen, *The Prologue to the Commentary on the Song of Songs*. Trans. Rowan A. Greer (Mahwah, New Jersey: The Paulist Press, 1979), p. 217.

29 See Inge, *Wanting Like a God*, pp. 28-37.

30 Ibid., p. 50.

> A Broken and a contrite heart is made up of knowledge
> Sorrow and Lov: knowledge of our primitive felicitie in
> Eden, Sorrow for our fall, Lov to God so Gratious and
> Redeeming. . . . Knowledge of the Joys prepared for us,
> Sorrow for our unworthiness in living beneath them, Lov to
> God for his Goodnesse Magnified and Exalted over us.[31]

Even in these early writings, Traherne manages to catch a tone that
is at once intimately private and yet also at the same time public – a
gift given to the real poet. And as a young man he was aware of the
insight granted to the innocence of the young child who sees the world
with the eyes of the soul, seeing inwardly (or imaginatively) as clearly
as outwardly. It is a gift that is too easily ground out of us as we grow
older. He writes:

> Till custom and Education had bred the Difference: it was as
> obvious to me to see all within us, as It was without. As easy
> and as natural to be Infinitly wide on the Inside, and to see all
> Kingdoms Times and persons within my Soul, as it is now to
> see them in the open world.[32]

And so I come in conclusion to what would have been one of
the most remarkable works in English literature and theology had
Traherne lived to complete it. Indeed, its completion would have been a
wonder of creation. Yet its very survival as we have it in a fragmentary
form is miraculous, for the *Commentaries of Heaven* was that work in
manuscript that was rescued, already alight, from the burning rubbish
heap in the 1960s, to be transported to Canada and then discovered
by pure accident twenty years later to be a work of Traherne. It was to
have been, when complete, an encyclopedia of theology in prose and
verse in celebration of the Mysteries of Felicitie. Even as it remains
it is on an enormous scale, such that, working in alphabetical order,
after four hundred pages of minute writing and ninety four entries
or 'commentaries', Traherne had got only as far in the alphabet as the
word 'Bastard'. Amongst the entries there is a wonderful poem of one
hundred and thirty seven lines on the term 'Affection'.

At the outset of the poem 'affections' are given physical characteristics
whereby the world created by God is to be felt and appreciated:

---

31 *Select Meditations*, I.93, *TTPP*, p. 78.
32 Ibid., III.27, *TTPP*, pp. 85-6.

Affections are the Wings and nimble feet
The Tongues by which we taste whats Good and Sweet.
The Armes by which a Spirit doth embrace,
Or thrust away; the Spurs which mend its Pace.
As Apprehensions are pure sparks of Light
Hands to lay hold on things, Ideas bright
Thoughts Sences or Intelligences.[33]

Traherne's verse is rapid, fluid, adaptable, exact and subtle, moving, as he had written of the child's perception, 'till custom and education had bred the difference', lodged between the external and the internal, the physical and the spiritual, without a moment's pause. And all is in celebration of that great act of love that is God's in the creation of the world and everything that is in it. It is a celebration in which time and eternity meet and each find the one in the other. Much of the poem is a lovely description of God seen through the glories of his creation - a 'Fountain of Delights', a 'Spring of Love a Spring of Bliss'. (There may here be an echo of the essay entitled 'The Translators to the Reader' that prefaces the King James Bible, where the words of Scripture are described as 'a fountain of most pure water springing up into everlasting life'.) Far from being a place that is afflicted by sin and the consequences of the Fall, this seemingly pre-lapsarian world is made 'to be a Scene of Love', a theatre in which God's majesty and power are acted out. As we aspire in our affections we come ever closer to God in our appreciation and participation in the joys of all creation, of which humankind, according to Genesis 1: 28, is the head and caretaker – Traherne would never have contradicted the word of the Bible:

His Peace and Joy is my Felicitie
In him alone is found another I
My Hope and Fear and Care and Grief and Joy
Them selvs about my Object to employ
He quickens all my Pow'rs, and is my Life,
While all the Creatures are at a great Strife
Who most should honor me. My Great Desires
And Hopes are Kindled only at his fires.
Theyr dead to all things else and ought to be
Only alive to their felicitie.

---

33 *The Works of Thomas Traherne*, Vol. II, pp. 293-4.

And that is God, who doth my Love regard
And that is God, who doth my Lov [*sic*] reward.[34]

Traherne, who seems quite naturally to move within the traditions of Christian mysticism, finds Christian love fulfilled in the divinization of humanity itself and yet never at the cost of his proper sense of humility, a true moment of *theosis*.

Traherne's poetry, recovered at least in part in our own day, it is true to say does not have the vital energy of Donne, the graceful fluidity of Herbert, or the faultless gentleness of Vaughan. Yet it has a voice that is quite unique in English poetry. As an Anglican priest Traherne lives, quite naturally, within the language world of the *Book of Common Prayer* and the King James Bible. He lives also, and almost unselfconsciously, within the broader structures of Christian theology, though without the Puritan emphasis on the redeeming love of Christ. For him it is God the creator, the source of all our want and felicitie and who has desired and loved his creation and all that is within it from the very beginning, who is first and foremost. Deeply and unapologetically Arminian in his outlook, Traherne's sense of the beauty of nature was bathed in sunlight and an awareness of the goodness of all things, never quite losing that childlike vision, or perhaps learning it again with proper wisdom, that sees both inwardly and outwardly – we might say that his intuitive imagination was as powerful as his sense of reality and reason. But Traherne would never dissociate these things and would say that this is to see with the eyes of the soul as much as with the eyes of the body. In his poetry, limited though it is in scope, words are transfigured, we might almost say redeemed with a deftness that in John Donne's verse is a deafening assault. Traherne is never coy – embracing and sanctifying all the joys of creation, including sex, and good wine and food. And love, at its best, is a two-way thing between God and humanity. God looks down upon our love for him, and rewards us with his love for us – which is, in Traherne's favourite word, true felicitie, or joy:

And that is God, who doth my Love regard
And that is God, who doth my Lov [*sic*] reward.

---

34 Ibid., p. 298.

Sir Philip Sidney
(1554-1586)

5.
Sir Philip Sidney:
High Matter in Noble Form

Sir Philip Sidney (1554-1586) seems to us today to be rather a remote and perhaps academic figure in English literature and history, though he is, in fact, a key person in what is known as the English Renaissance. I would be surprised if many of my readers had encountered that much of his work or perhaps even have heard much about him, but I find that he is another poet whom I have been reading almost all my life and in his quaintness he is dear to me. I have known him much longer than I have known Traherne. In literature and in his poetics Sidney looks back to the stylized courtly poetry of the late Middle Ages and at the same time he looks forward to the plays and poems of William Shakespeare, on whom he was a considerable influence, and then further into the seventeenth century Anglican metaphysical poet George Herbert and indeed to Thomas Traherne, the subject of the previous chapter. The great John Donne, poet and Dean of St Paul's Cathedral in London, where Sidney was buried, described the translations of the Psalms by Sidney and his sister Mary, the Countess of Pembroke, now known as the *Sidney Psalter*, and with which I shall be largely concerned in this chapter, as 'the highest matter in the noblest form'.[1] In history the

---

1   John Donne, 'Upon the Translation of the Psalms by Sir Philip Sidney, and the Countess of Pembroke His Sister', line 11, in *The Sidney Psalter*, ed. by Hannibal

nobly born Philip Sidney was a key figure in the court and politics of
Queen Elizabeth I, his career cut short at the age of thirty-two when he
was mortally wounded on military service in the Netherlands. He was
buried with great ceremony in London's Cathedral.

As a poet and writer Sidney has enjoyed mixed fortunes over the
years and centuries. I would not expect anyone today, apart from
professional scholars, to spend much time reading either his prose or
his verse. Even in his own time the legend of him as a courtier and a
solder grew more than that of him as a man of letters. And it was in
about 1610 that Sir Fulke Greville, with the 'collaboration and approval'
of the Sidney family, made famous the manner of Sidney's death and his
final words in battle, it being written that:

> being thirstie with excess of bleeding, he called for drink,
> which was presently brought him; but as he was putting the
> bottle to his mouth, he saw a poor Souldier carryed along,
> who had eaten his last at the same Feast, gastly casting up his
> eyes at the bottle. Which Sir *Philip* perceiving, took it from
> his head, before he drank, and delivered it to the poor man,
> with these words, *Thy necessity is yet greater than mine.* And
> when he had pledged this poor souldier, he was presently
> carried to *Arnheim*.[2]

But by the middle of the eighteenth century Sidney's prestige as a
poet and writer had reached rock bottom. In a famous passage the
novelist Horace Walpole described Sidney's prose work the *Arcadia* as
'a tedious, lamentable, pedantic pastoral romance, which the patience
of a young virgin in love cannot now wade through'. As a poet, Sidney
fared no better, making, says Walpole, 'some absurd attempts to fetter
English verse in Roman chains; a proof that this applauded author
understood little of the genius of his own language'.[3]

So – with that rather unhelpful encouragement let us now turn our
attention to Sidney himself and allow me to try and persuade you that
Walpole got it quite wrong! Sidney, born at Penshurst in Kent, spent
his life amongst the nobility of England and in the Court of Queen

---

Hamlin, Michael G. Brennan, Margaret P. Hannay and Noel J. Kinnamon
(Oxford: Oxford University Press, 2009), p. 3. (Henceforth cited as *SP*)

2   Fulke Greville, *The Life of the Renowned Sir Philip Sidney* (1652), quoted in Martin
Garrett, *Sidney: The Critical Heritage* (London: Routledge, 2015), pp. 192-3.

3   Horace Walpole, *A Catalogue of the Royal and Noble Authors of England* (1758),
quoted in Garrett, op. cit. p. 286.

Elizabeth I. He was educated at Shrewsbury School and Corpus Christi College, Oxford. He did not take a degree at university as that then was regarded as a somewhat ungentlemanly thing to do, smacking rather of the tradesman. Sidney then spent some years on the Grand Tour of Europe, becoming proficient in a number of languages, both ancient and modern, and preparing for a life that was at once literary and also spent in diplomatic and military service to the Queen. Sidney was the supreme example of a 'Renaissance man' – a learned and broadly cultured person, well read in the classics and classical rhetoric, a scholarly type that is sadly largely unknown in today's highly specialised world. He was perfectly capable of writing poetry not only in English but also Latin, Greek and even Hebrew. He knew a little of everything and a great deal about some things. Like everyone else in his age, Sidney was, at least in our terms, a deeply religious man – an urbane Protestant and servant of Queen Elizabeth. But I doubt if he would have regarded himself as an exceptionally religious personality. It was just that religion and Christianity then permeated everything. As we will see shortly, translating the Psalms was something of a preoccupation amongst poets of the time, but the *Sidney Psalter*, a joint work of Sidney and his sister Mary, Countess of Pembroke, stands apart as a work of literature and spirituality and in profound contrast, as will become evident, to the more familiar Psalms of the *Book of Common Prayer* (by Miles Coverdale [1488-1569]) and composed, of course, before the appearance of the King James Version of the Bible in 1611. Like many high-class works at that time, the *Sidney Psalter* was not actually published, but circulated quite widely in manuscript form within a certain controlled group of readers. It was a psalter intended for private prayer and in a moment we will read some of these poems or psalms alongside the more familiar and 'public' Psalter of the *Book of Common Prayer* of the English Church.

Sidney was also a poet saturated in the humanistic spirit of his age, learned not only in the Greek and Latin classics, but also contemporary Italian literature and art (the great Italian philosopher Giordano Bruno dedicated one of his works to him), and the product of a gentlemanly education that was founded upon the courtly ideals expressed in such works as Sir Thomas Elyot's hugely influential *The Book of the Governor* (1531). Elyot's book, which Shakespeare knew well, was a work of philosophy dedicated to the new political theory of the age, to moral philosophy and to the principles of education, in short everything linked to religion and the manners that flowed down from the life of the royal court. At the heart of all of these principles was a thorough training in the art of rhetoric, understood not in the rather narrow modern sense but after the classical model, known especially through the work of Cicero, whereby *language*, in all its careful and carefully constructed nuances, was the root of learning and moral training in 'virtue'. How we speak or write is what we are. This last quality of 'virtue' is central if we are to understand Sidney and his age. In its classical origins, virtue was a specifically manly quality, derived from the Latin word *vir*, meaning 'man', and denoting such qualities as bravery in battle and loyalty to one's comrades in arms. In its later Christian form, virtue became a much broader moral quality, more gentle and embracing every ethical quality in life under God and before one's fellow human beings. Such was the nature of Sidney's preoccupation with virtue, which as 'Lady Vertue' becomes feminine in gender in his work *The Defence of Poesy* (written, 1579-80).[4]

It is not perhaps entirely surprising that I was introduced to the works of Philip Sidney when I was at school, creeping like a snail unwillingly each day to an establishment not entirely unlike Sidney's own Shrewsbury School and one that was founded in 1619 as Dulwich College, not so very long after his time, though by my time its values were perhaps more informed by the muscular Christianity of the Victorian age than the Christian humanism of the English Renaissance. But yet there were still remaining the last remnants of an education as known to Sidney yet lingering in the English air of the public school even in the middle years of the twentieth century. It may be different now. We, it has to be said, very rarely read Sidney's translations of the Psalms, but we did occasionally read his two major works, in poetry *Astrophel and Stella* (1591), and, in prose, *The Arcadia* (1593), together with his major treatise on the theory of poetry, *The Defence of Poesy*, sometimes known as *An Apology for Poetry* (published posthumously in 1595). All of these writings are hard work for today's reader, as indeed they had been for the reader even in the eighteenth century, though the sonnet sequence *Astrophel and Stella*, with its interleaved songs, stands easily alongside Shakespeare's great sequence of one hundred and fifty-four *Sonnets* (1609) and Edmund Spenser's *The Shepherd's Calendar* (1579) – which, like *Astrophel*, is rooted in Virgil's *Eclogues* as well as Theocritus – as a pinnacle of English Renaissance literary achievement.

---

4   See further, Warner Berthoff, *Literature and the Continuances of Virtue* (Princeton: Princeton University Press, 1986), p. 53.

They are not easy to read but they do repay the effort required to attend to them for a number of reasons. Sidney's sonnet sequence is, first of all, an almost perfect example of Petrarchan poetry, after the model of the Italian early Renaissance poet Francesco Petrarch (1304-74), and thus indicative of Sidney's profoundly European culture. He would certainly not have approved of Brexit in any form! (Actually you cannot really understand the poetry of the Anglican *Book of Common Prayer* without knowing something of the poetry of Petrarch, though liturgists in the church rarely acknowledge or even realise this).[5] Second, the one hundred and eight sonnets and eleven songs of *Astrophel and Stella* explore in minute detail the necessary and tortuous relationship between love and that all-important notion of *virtue*. And finally, only William Shakespeare outshines Sidney in the balance between highly disciplined poetic forms and the natural rhythms and patterns of everyday language – Sidney created a 'voice' that is capable of exploring precisely and clearly the complete range of the profound complexities of human emotions, thoughts and feelings. This is a skill in words that, by and large, we have lost in our over-technologized age with its crass simplification of language and vocabulary. Indeed we have very largely lost the delicate art of using words precisely in poetry. Consider for example Sonnet 10 from *Astrophel* where Sidney, playing also with the language of religion and biblical imagery, addresses 'reason' as it argues against the fooleries of love, and asks rather that reason instead support his love for Stella. The old word 'brabbling' here means brawling:

> Reason, in faith thou art well serv'd, that still
> Would brabbling be with sense and love in me;
> I rather wish'd thee climb the Muses' hill;
> Or reach the fruit of Nature's choicest tree;
> Or seek heaven's course or heaven's inside to see.
> Why shouldst thou toil our thorny soil to till?[6]

Sidney, in short, eloquently expresses his impatience with that age-old injunction of age to youth, that it 'be reasonable'. But when reason itself sees Stella, so it too is, and for good reason, utterly defeated by her beauty:

---

5   See, David Jasper, *The Language of Liturgy* (London: SCM, 2018), pp. 39-42.
6   Sir Philip Sidney, *Selected Prose and Poetry*, ed. by Robert Kimbrough. (New York: Holt, Rinehart and Winston, 1969), p. 168.

For, soon as they strake thee with Stella's rays,
   Reason, thou kneel'dst, and offer'dst straight to prove,
   By reason good, good reason her to love.[7]

Language was in Sidney's day a delicate instrument of expression drawing upon all the resources of Renaissance rhetoric. Words make us think and work hard in the process of understanding. They are, as Coleridge was later to insist, living things. It is in his treatise *The Defence of Poesy* that Sidney explores at length what he means by *reason* – it was to become something very different in the eighteenth century. For him in the late sixteenth century the reason which resides in the rational soul is nothing other than the element of the divine that is within each of us. Its origin is God himself, who is the creator of all things – and thus the poet is, after God and above all, a *maker*, the creator of poetry literally out of nothing. This term has, of course, been more recently revived in Scotland since 2002 with the appointment of the publicly funded poet, the Edinburgh *Makar*.[8] The poet is one who is inspired – that is, breathed into by the divine breath – and poetry, writes Sidney, 'ever sets virtue out in her best colours', and (thinking back to the love sonnets of *Astrophel and Stella*) 'making fortune her well-waiting handmaid, that one must needs be enamored of her.'[9]

The poet, Sidney maintains, must be utterly immersed in his art with an integrity that he calls, in Latin (derived from the Greek), *energia*, or 'forcibleness'. *The Defence of Poesy*, which is deliberately composed in a Ciceronian manner as a formal lesson or oration, finds poetry, in both the Greek writings of Homer and the Hebrew Psalms of David, to lie at the very basis of our civilisation. The ancient poet was a 'Vates' or prophetic figure long before philosophy was ever dreamed of. Consequently the poet is one who 'deserveth not to be scourged out of the Church of God'.[10] We should bear that in mind today! The poetry of

---

7   Ibid.

8   Further Scottish Makars were appointed in 2004, in Glasgow, Stirling and Dundee. It was originally specifically used to refer to a group of late medieval and early Renaissance poets in the fifteenth and sixteenth centuries in Scotland, especially Robert Henryson, William Dunbar and Gavin Douglas.

9   Sir Philip Sidney, *The Defence of Poesy* [1595], reprinted, ed. by Edmund D. Jones, *English Critical Essays, XVI– XVIII Centuries* (Oxford: Oxford University Press, 1965), p. 19. (Jones adopts the alternative title of the work, *An Apology for Poetry*.)

10 Ibid., p. 6.

the Psalms literally brings things into being in the imagination, Sidney noting the poet King David (who was, for him, their author), in 'his notable *prosopopeias* [personifications] when he maketh you, as it were, see God coming in his majesty, his telling of the beasts' joyfulness, and hills leaping'. And what is this 'but a heavenly poesy, wherein he almost showeth himself a passionate lover of that unspeakable and everlasting beauty to be seen by the eyes of the mind, only cleared by faith'.[11] The poets of the Bible, Sidney goes on, with all reasonableness, 'were they that did imitate the unconceivable excellencies of God'. Even Jesus Christ himself employed the arts of poetry in his teachings as recorded in the gospels.

As you would expect of a Renaissance classical scholar like Sidney, his chief guide to the nature of poetry is the Greek philosopher Aristotle in his foundational work the *Poetics*. It is here that we are taught that poetry is a teacher superior to history, for if history refers but to the particular, the historian being 'loaden with old mouse-eaten records',[12] then poetry soars towards the universal through the reason of divine inspiration. And it is poetry that 'ever sets virtue so out in her best colours, making fortune her well-waiting handmaid, that one needs must be enamoured of her'.[13] It is in *The Defence* that we find the familiar words, 'now, for the poet, he nothing affirmeth, and therefore never lieth'. Unlike the historian, who is forever harping on about the truth in facts, 'the poet never maketh any circles about your imagination, to conjure you to believe for true what he writeth'.[14] In the Bible, Nathan, when he tells his parable of the lamb to catch the conscience of King David after his adultery with Bathsheba, does not intend that his fable be taken as a reporting of facts. Rather it acts like a mirror to David himself, with whom the truth of the matter actually rests. That is how poetry and stories work. Prospero's speech at the very end of Shakespeare's *Tempest* is an acknowledgement that the poet – Prospero or Shakespeare (they are, perhaps, to be understood here as one and the same) – conjures up worlds in our minds which we may choose willingly to enter or not: but those worlds *matter* most profoundly, as in *Hamlet*, in the play within the play, they hold up a mirror to nature that is capable of exposing the moral and spiritual truths of ourselves. The poet never lies, though you can opt to ignore him or

11 Ibid.
12 Ibid., p. 12.
13 Ibid., p. 19.
14 Ibid., p. 33.

her, as the rich young man in Matthew 19: 16-22 chose to ignore Jesus for the cost of the truth to him was too high. But Hamlet's play within a play, *The Mousetrap*, like Nathan's parable with David, catches the conscience of the king, Claudius, more effectively than any reasoned argument. The very words of the play bite into his guilty soul.

Sidney concludes *The Defence of Poesy* with a lovely phrase regarding the 'planet-like music of poetry'. It is a reference to the ancient belief in the *musica universalis* – the harmonious music of the circling spheres. Do 'you have so earth-creeping a mind that it cannot lift itself up to look to the sky of poetry?' Sidney asks, ending with the wish that 'while you live, you live in love, and never get favour for lacking the skill of a Sonnet, and, when you die, your memory die from the earth for want of an Epitaph'.[15] We should never neglect poetry.

And so we move on to the *Sidney Psalter*. Sidney died in battle, still a young man and at the time of his death only forty-three psalm translations had been completed. His devoted sister Mary, the Countess of Pembroke, in her way as fine a poet as Philip himself, completed the full canon of one hundred and fifty psalms, and probably revised and contributed to some of Philip's earlier poems as well – certainly she edited his translation of Psalm 1. These are very much poems of their time and often not easy for us to read. As I have said, Sidney and his sister also were trained in what was known as classical rhetoric, a formal use of language that loves to indulge in complex word-play and what are known as tropes with lovely names – metaphors, metonymy, synechdoche, irony, paradox, litotes, prosopopeia, and so on. Modern English has ironed out much of this riddling richness in our doubtful pursuit of the literal and the straightforward. As we march, blindly, towards the 'newspeak' of George Orwell's *1984* (Donald Trump's crass illiteracy in his speeches is a prime example – and indicative of the post-truth dangers of over-simplification and sheer bad grammar), we forget, or, I suspect, have often simply become too lazy to appreciate, the fine linguistic instrument with which Philip and Mary explore the human soul in their own music of the Psalms.

Psalm translation was something of a fashion in the Renaissance, flourishing in France and Italy before a late flowering in English in the sixteenth century, so that the poet and priest John Donne still lamented that 'Psalms are become so well attired abroad, so ill at home'.[16] But gradually

---

15 Ibid., pp. 53-4.
16 John Donne, 'Upon the Translation of the Psalms by Sir Philip Sidney, and the Countess of Pembroke His Sister', lines 37-8, in *SP*, p. 4.

English psalm translations begin to abound, by, among others, Sir Thomas Wyatt, George Gascoigne, Richard Stanyhurst and many more. The metrical Psalms of Thomas Sternhold and John Hopkins were first published in full in 1562, set to music in 1556, and by 1640 about three hundred editions of them had been published. The *Sidney Psalter* was, as I have already noted, never published but circulated in hand-written manuscripts (a not uncommon phenomenon in those days), yet was widely popular and had an enormous influence on subsequent English poetry, including, as we shall see, the verse of George Herbert, John Milton and many others. Often underestimated by later literary critics, the poetry of these Psalm translations is highly sophisticated and original, each poem in a different metre or stanza form. No less a personage than John Donne wrote a long dedicatory poem to the work extolling the virtues of these 'Sidneian Psalms' and the 'sweet learned labours' of Philip and his sister Mary.[17]

The poetic music of *The Sidney Psalter* is very different from the much earlier tones of what is for most of us the far more familiar music of the Coverdale psalms of the *Book of Common Prayer*, glorious though that is, and still more or less reproduced in a more modern form in our books of daily offices or in the Church of England's current liturgy known as *Common Worship*. Miles Coverdale's (1488-1568) psalms were written for corporate worship, to be said or sung together in church, but Sidney's paraphrases of the Psalms serve a rather different devotional purpose. They are complex and meditative poems to be read, and perhaps prayed, privately and in solitude – or possibly very occasionally sung as songs. They lack the economy and occasional terseness of our more familiar liturgical Psalter, but they require us to linger and reflect within different rhyming forms that can take a while to 'hear' and get used to. More than just translations, they are original poems in their own right. Here is the second stanza of Philip's poem of Psalm 1 which was revised by Mary after his death:

> He shall be like a freshly planted tree
>   To which sweet springs of water neighbours be,
> Whose branches fail not timely fruit to nourish,
>   Nor withered leaf shall make it fail to flourish.
> So all the things whereto that man doth bend,
>   Shall prosper still, with well-succeeding end.[18]

---

17 Ibid., pp. 3-4.
18 *SP*. p. 11.

What strikes me about this careful rhyming verse is how it slows us down. The words are carefully, deliberately used in rhythm and will not be hurried. The last two lines about 'that man', the *beatus vir*, or the man of virtue, who is the subject of the whole Psalm, sit, as it were, under the shade of the image of the growing, fruitful tree – linked merely by the one word 'so'.

Here is the opening stanza of the poem of Psalm 4 – entitled in Latin by Sidney, as in the *Prayer Book*, '*Cum invocarem*':

> Hear me, oh, hear me, when I call,
>> O God, God of my equity:
>> Thou sett'st me free when I was thrall,
>> Have mercy still on me,
>> And harken how I pray to thee.[19]

Now read aloud and listen to the more familiar Coverdale version from the *Prayer Book*: 'Hear me when I call, O God of my righteousness: thou hast set me at liberty when I was in trouble; have mercy upon me, and hearken unto my prayer.' Sidney, who would have been perfectly familiar with the Coverdale version in the Elizabethan *Prayer Book* of 1559,[20] and whose poetry often indeed reflects its rhythms and language, chooses to go in an entirely different direction with his poem. In contrast to Coverdale's flowing syntax, he chooses a halting, hesitant, almost stammering rhythm, disrupted by repetition – 'Hear me, oh, hear me . . . O God, God . . .'. The invocation to God becomes a slow, rather painful, pleading prayer, and it continues in like manner, using all the devices of word-play beloved of the Renaissance poet, until we reach the last verse in which all the hesitations and disruptions are finally resolved in a poetry of flowing sweetness:

> So I in peace and peaceful bliss
>> Will lay me down and take my rest:
>> For it is thou Lord, thou it is,
>> By pow'r of whose own only breast
>> I dwell, laid up in safest nest.[21]

---

19 Ibid., p. 14.

20 The Act for the Uniformity of Common Prayer that prefaced the 1559 *Prayer Book* required that all 'persons inhabiting within this realm' attend church on pain of punishment by fine.

21 *SP*. p. 15.

Throughout Sidney is in perfect control of both language and verse.

There are moments in *The Sidney Psalter* when its influence upon the later and now much better known poetry of George Herbert is plain enough. It was, indeed, the model for Herbert's work *The Temple* (1633), which contains most of Herbert's surviving English poems. Philip and Mary as well as Herbert are aware that words are powerful not simply because of what they *mean*, but because of what they *do*, even how they appear on the page, and how they affect us in sound and metre. Poems are living things. In Psalm 13, Sidney tightens up the syntax of the *Prayer Book* (echoed in the later King James Version) to give us a cry of anguish to God, each line broken by a brief three syllable cry of pain that is resolved only in the last two couplets: 'What? Ever?; Dissever; In anguish; Thus languish; My crying; In dying; Prevailèd; Assailèd; Great pity; Song's ditty'. The opening of Sidney's poem is as dramatic as anything in his translation of the Psalms:

> How long (O Lord) shall I forgotten be?
> > What? Ever?
> How long wilt thou thy hidden face from me
> > Dissever?[22]

Sidney subtly changes the *Prayer Book* sense of that last cry. Coverdale simply has it as 'How long wilt thou turn thy face away from me?' Sidney places the action one step further back. God is not turning his face away, *he has already done so*, so that his is a 'hidden face' from which we are already separated (or 'dissevered'). Language and syntax, then, was carefully used.

One of my favourite Sidney psalms is 14 – known to us as the Psalm that begins with the words 'The fool hath said in his heart . . .' – *Dixit insipiens*. Sidney allows himself to develop and expand this to 'The foolish man by flesh and fancy led'. But it is the fifth verse that shows us Sidney as a poet of his own time and culture:

> O madness of these folks, thus loosely led!
> > These cannibals, who, as if they were bread
> > God's people do devour.[23]

The Coverdale version in the *Prayer Book* has the much simpler, 'eating up my people as it were bread.' Sidney is bringing in here a highly topical and wholly un-biblical term in describing these 'workers

---

22 Ibid., p. 28.
23 Ibid., p. 29.

of mischief' as cannibals. The first recorded use of this term in English is in 1553, the 'Canibales' (a Spanish word) being the name given to a fierce tribe in the fairly recently discovered West Indies, and a derivative from the broadly ethnic term for the local peoples 'Caribes' (from which, of course, comes the name Caribbean). The propensity of these people to eat human flesh seems to have exercised a revolted fascination upon the Elizabethan age – and Sidney brings this current obsession into the biblical Psalm with powerful effect.

But I cannot pass without some further mention of Mary Sidney, Countess of Pembroke, who is actually the author of more than half of *The Sidney Psalter* and one of the great women poets writing in English. She has not been given her proper due.[24] Even more than Philip she weaves into her psalm poems the life and culture of the Elizabethan court, but perhaps her greatest and certainly best known achievement is her Psalm 139 – *Domine, probasti*. In the Coverdale version it begins with the words, 'O Lord, though hast searched me out, and known me'. In Mary Sidney's poem this becomes one of the most acute investigations into the intricacies of the human heart and mind before God in English poetry. Before we look at stanza 8 of her poem, here is Coverdale's translation (Psalm 139: 14): 'My bones are not hid from thee: though I be made secretly, and fashioned beneath in the earth'.

Now Mary Sidney:

> Thou how my back was beam-wise laid
>   And raft'ring of my ribs dost know:
>   Know'st every point
>   Of bone and joint,
>   How to this whole these parts did grow,
> In brave embroid'ry fair arrayed,
>   Though wrought in shop both dark and low.[25]

Mary adds and develops a powerful architectural metaphor to describe the creation of her body, using alliteration (back/beam-wise; raft'ring/ribs) to emphasise the hammering of the roof's construction. She then shifts to another metaphor, this time from embroidery – the body not 'fashioned beneath in the earth' as Coverdale expresses it, but more precisely like

---

24 A biography of the Countess of Pembroke was published in 1990 written by Margaret Hannay. Entitled *Philip's Phoenix*, it is hard to come by but very well worth a read.

25 *SP*. p. 269.

a beautiful tapestry that is created and sewn in a dark and noisome Elizabethan workshop. This is indeed subtle, allusive and original writing, as complex and inward as anything in Shakespeare himself.

The Sidneys' poetic adaptations and meditations on the Psalms, with their psychological realism, their dramatic separation of the sinful from the righteous and their clear presentation of the Psalms as Christian poems and prayers to a benevolent God, were, as I have suggested, only privately circulated in their time, though they moved in the highest circles as the Countess of Pembroke presented a copy to Queen Elizabeth I herself in 1599. Mary, who married into an aristocratic class beyond the reach of Philip himself, was a considerable patron of literature, admired, among others, by the poet Edmund Spenser, and only in our own time is she slowly beginning to recover the readership which she deserves. It was not until 1823 that these prayers (for that is really what the Sidney Psalms are), composed for the private room or chapel, finally found their way into printed publication. Perhaps they do not suit the modern demand for originality, but that was not the ethos of their time, for as their most recent editors have commented:

> The *Psalms* of Philip and Mary Sidney are among the greatest translations in Renaissance poetry, 'unoriginal' in that the 'original' matter is biblical, but highly 'original' in the way they artfully turn the biblical Psalms into uniquely English poems.[26]

Furthermore, as the fruit of Renaissance learning, and often chivalric and courtly in tone, the Sidney Psalms also anticipate the preoccupations of the seventeenth and eighteenth centuries in sometimes extraordinary ways. In Psalm 19 Philip Sidney writes of the Book of Nature by which, alongside the Bible – the other Book - the works of God are read. (More familiarly we might think of the nineteenth century poem on the Book of Nature, still occasionally sung as a hymn, by John Keble from *The Christian Year* [1827] – 'There is a book who runs may read.') Sidney writes:

> There be no eyne, but read the line
>   From so fair book proceeding:
> Their words be set in letters great
>   For everybody's reading.[27]

---

26 *SP*, Introduction, p. xxix.
27 *SP*. p. 37.

Sir Philip Sidney, one senses, was a gentle and well-mannered soul; perhaps 'courtly' would be a better description. In any event, and despite his soldierly death in Arnheim, with his famous, noble last words on the other soldier's greater need, he does not portray rage or anger well in his poetry. Rather, he is fascinated by the endless play of words in double meanings, ironies, subtle jokes – a true metaphysical like Donne, Herbert and Traherne after him – teasing the brain into a nice awareness of the delicacy and complexity of prayer. He was, it could be said, a simple, complicated man. If our own age has a deadly tendency towards the anti-intellectual, Sidney, together with his formidable sister, perhaps, tend towards the opposite – though that is, I would suggest, no bad thing. Here is a typically brilliant example of what rhetoricians call *onomasia* (the use of words that sound alike placed together) in Psalm 38. One realises here that this is poetry to be seen and read rather than spoken and heard – where the visual word-play of reins/reigns/remains would to an extent be lost:

> In my reins hot torments reignes,
>   There remains
>   Nothing in my body sound.
>   I am weak and broken sore,
>   Yea, I roar,
> In my heart such grief is found.[28]

There are no such subtleties in the *Prayer Book*, Coverdale Version:

> For my loins are filled with a sore disease: and there is no whole part in my body.
>   I am feeble and sore smitten: I have roared for the very disquietness of my heart. (Psalm 38: 7-8).

While the Coverdale's psalm pulls no punches with its savage, direct imagery, Sidney remains ever the courtier, the wordsmith whose roaring 'in my heart' hardly convinces, yet still is deeply felt.

Sidney died, by our standards, a young man, barely beyond thirty, though he was in his own time thought of as already into middle age. His *Psalter* remained incomplete, indeed unedited by him, the intimate prayers of a Renaissance Christian humanist. Although his reputation as a courtier, soldier, writer and poet was in his own time considerable, he is now utterly overshadowed by the mighty contemporary figure

---

28 *SP*. p. 74.

of William Shakespeare, and later by the metaphysical poetry of his admirers John Donne, George Herbert, Thomas Traherne and Henry Vaughan. Unlike both Donne and Herbert, Sidney was no theologian and he never pretended to be. His universe under a generally benevolent God (and it would probably never have occurred to him not to regard the biblical Psalms as anything other than Christian songs, though he knew them also in Hebrew) was actually fairly simple in concept, far more so than that of Traherne, based upon the courtly, Renaissance principles of virtue, love and honour. Yet Sidney's riddling explorations of the human situation are precise and delicate, before God in the *Sidney Psalter* and in matters of erotic love in *Astrophel and Stella*. It is true that it is difficult today to read his rather lush and verbose prose work *Arcadia*, a kind of proto-novel, with any degree of enjoyment, though it takes its place in English literature as heroic drama, a polished portrait of a lost world of chivalric romance. But in his theories of the power of poetry in *The Defence of Poesy*, and in his graceful adaptations of the Psalms, Sidney still calls our attention to an age when England and Europe were emerging from the long, dark Middle Ages into a period of bright intellectual ferment and cultural change that heralded, in the far distance, modernity and our own times. At the end of the sixteenth century change was taking place not least in the matter of religion which still then permeated every element of life and culture at all levels. Within Sidney's lifetime the Archbishop of Canterbury, Thomas Cranmer, the principal architect of the *Book of Common Prayer* that first appeared in 1549, was burnt as a martyr in Oxford by the Roman Catholic Queen Mary, and it was a time when to hold a suspect theological doctrine could well cost you your life. The 1559 *Book of Common Prayer* of Queen Elizabeth I was a masterpiece of learned Anglican compromise, the result of very much the same schooling enjoyed by Sidney himself and the *Prayer Book* of a Queen who was herself no mean scholar, a classicist who read Isocrates and Cicero, was learned in no less than five languages, and knew her theology from St Cyprian to Philip Melanchthon.[29] Shakespeare was born (or at least baptised) in 1564, when Sidney was ten years old, though into a very different and far less privileged sphere of life, an upstart crow. I suspect that neither Sidney nor Shakespeare would be thought of today as particularly religious men – the one absorbed in

---

29 See, John E. Booty, Ed. *The Book of Common Prayer (1559): The Elizabethan Prayer Book* (Charlottesville: The University of Virginia Press, 2005), p. 332.

his career as a diplomat, courtier, soldier and poet of courtly love, the other a working man of the theatre who never thought of publishing his plays. But for both of them, the matter of Christianity and its sense of virtue, its dangers and its glories, is never far away, and it is entwined in their visions of life in a complex, changing world where 'wit' was honoured, virtue treasured and words bit deeply and were held dear. I end with the conclusion of Sidney's Psalm 23, not because I think it is great poetry, or even Sidney (edited by Mary) at his best, but because it is, to us with our doubts and general cultural lack of concern for poetry, so odd. It seems strange with its wordplays, its experiments with verse and rhythm and, perhaps, its absolute assumption of the love of God in Christ. It is a song, and should at least be read, or, in this case, better sung, like all of the Psalms:

> Thou oil'st my head, thou fill'st my cup:
>   Nay more, thou endless good,
>   Shalt give me food.
> To thee, I say, ascended up,
>   Where thou the Lord of all,
>   Dost hold thy hall.[30]

In the tone and sense of language here in this Psalm we can see how Sidney's verse fed and tutored that of George Herbert who was, perhaps, in the end, the greater poet. Here is the end of Herbert's Psalm 23 from his work *The Temple*:

> My head with oil, my cup with wine
>   Runs over night and day.
>
> Surely thy sweet and wondrous love
>   Shall measure all my days;
> And as it never shall remove,
>   So neither shall my praise.[31]

It is an appropriate moment to end this chapter, as we move now to a poet of our own time, also a 'metaphysical' in his way – Sir Geoffrey Hill.

---

30 *SP*. p. 45.
31 Donald Davie, (Ed.) *The Psalms in English* (Harmondsworth: Penguin, 1996), p. 118.

Geoffrey Hill
(1932-2016)

6.
Geoffrey Hill:
The Strange Flesh Untouched

While all who attend to fiddle or to harp
For betterment, flavour their decent mouths
With gobbets of the sweetest sacrifice.[1]
(Geoffrey Hill)

I have left myself with possibly the most difficult task to accomplish as I begin to draw towards the end of this little book on poetry and religion. Sir Geoffrey Hill is, arguably, the greatest of contemporary English poets (he died in 2016), but also one of the most elusive and remains little read, I suspect, outside a fairly narrow coterie of academics and stalwart poetry lovers. It is not very surprising as he is a very difficult writer indeed. I never met him myself, which I particularly regret as, like myself (though he was far more distinguished), he was a professor of literature and religion, he being so at Boston University, Massachusetts before returning to Cambridge, England towards the end of his life. But I have friends who knew him well, and attest to his dark, depressive character, his brilliance, his awkwardness and impatience. The late and saintly Peter Walker, a classical scholar, former Bishop of Ely and the bishop who ordained me deacon in 1976 – we will return to Peter later

---

1   Geoffrey Hill, 'Annunciations' (1), in *King Log* (London: André Deutsche, 1968), p. 14.

as he appears in Hill's poem *The Triumph of Love* – shared Hill's taste for careful, classical, labyrinthine syntax and understood something of the profound Christian spirituality that was deep in his dark soul. Reading Hill's poetry is in some ways rather like what it was to listen to one of Bishop Peter's sermons. At the time you wonder what on earth they are about, but their phrases and images come back later to haunt you and somehow you know that something strange and new has been revealed, most often in contradictions or irony.

We have two books of essays by Geoffrey Hill, *The Lords of Limit* (1984) and *The Enemy's Country* (1991). They are difficult to read, stylistically challenging, but infinitely rewarding if persevered with, and perhaps the best places to begin in any attempt at trying to understand Hill. He writes with a careful, minute precision of language that is rare for us, learning from the writings of Sir Philip Sidney and the poets of the seventeenth century, and finally the Romantic poet and thinker Samuel Taylor Coleridge for whom, Hill likes to remind us (as if you needed it in this book), words are 'not THINGS, they are LIVING POWERS, by which the things of most importance to mankind are actuated, combined, and humanized'.[2] Words and sentences from Hill's pen burn with an ethical and grammatical nicety that does not yield to understanding immediately, but rewards careful persistence. He begins his essay 'Our Word Is Our Bond'[3] with a reference to Sir Philip Sidney's familiar statement about the poet, which we have already encountered in *The Defence of Poesy*, that 'he nothing affirmeth, and therefore never lieth'. Sidney, Hill remarks, 'as shrewd as he was magnanimous, evidently had it in mind to keep poetry out of the courts'.[4] The analogy with Hill's argument that immediately springs to my mind is the Pauline distinction between law and grace. Poetry lives by grace, a gift that flourishes within the beautiful, the suggestive, the oblique. As another poet, the American Emily Dickinson, once famously remarked, 'Tell all the Truth but tell it slant – Success in Circuit lies'.[5] In 'Our Word Is Our Bond', Hill sets poetry up against the bleak linguistic positivism

---

2   S.T. Coleridge, Preface to *Aids to Reflection*, rev. edn. 1896, quoted in Geoffrey Hill, *The Lords of Limit: Essays on Literature and Ideas* (London: André Deutsche, 1984), p. 91.

3   Hill, *The Lords of Limit*, pp. 138-59. First published in *Agenda*, Vol. 21, no. 1 (Spring, 1983).

4   Ibid., p. 138.

5   Emily Dickinson, *The Complete Poems*, ed. by Thomas H. Johnson (London: Faber and Faber, 1970), p. 506. The line was used for the title of a book of sermons by that deeply underrated scholar of literature and theology, the late Bishop John Tinsley, *Tell it Slant* [1979] (Indiana: Wyndham Hall Press, 1990).

of J.L. Austin's famous book *How To Do Things With Words* (1962), claiming a precision of a different kind in poetry, and reminding us, with typical refinement, that Sidney (adjusting the thought of Aristotle) claims that poetry is greater than either philosophy or history, combining the wisdom of the one with the particularity of the other.[6]

Theology and the matter of religion permeate almost all of Geoffrey Hill's writings and poetry. He returns again and again to the work of the great Scottish theologian Donald MacKinnon, knowing that the business of poetry and religion is anything but straightforward, though ideally, he once remarked, his theme would be perfectly simple, an act of atonement:

> the technical perfecting of a poem is an act of atonement, in the radical etymological sense – an act of at-one-ment, a setting at one, a bringing into concord, a reconciling, a uniting in harmony.[7]

But, of course, it never can be that simple. Hill worries over a nice distinction that is worth a moment's reflection, looking back with a typical literary reference (Hill, like Coleridge, seems to have read everything) to Helen Waddell's novel *Peter Abelard*, in which one character remarks that 'one can repent and be absolved of a sin, but there is no canonical repentance for a mistake.' In the same way, as G.K. Chesterton once said, 'There are ways of getting absolved for a murder; there are no ways of getting absolved for upsetting the soup.'[8] I think, perhaps, that in our own lives the mistakes worry us much more than the occasional spectacular sins, and their stains are somehow much harder to eradicate. The church, certainly, has no idea what to do about them.

Is this, maybe, one reason why we have become so distant from modern poetry – or perhaps it is the other way round? It is just too distant, too high class. As Hill expressed it of T.S. Eliot, thinking of Eliot's later rather remote plays like *The Confidential Clerk* (1954) and *The Elder Statesman* (1959), he 'could genuinely mistake "the fashionable requirements" of Shaftesbury Avenue or the Edinburgh Festival for the needs of "a wider audience".'[9] Poetry for us, it may be, has become separated from its wider audience, that is people like ourselves who are so harassed and beset by our endless, daily, upsetting mistakes even more, perhaps, than our grave

---

6   *The Lords of Limit*, p. 144.
7   Ibid., p. 2.
8   Quoted in *The Lords of Limit*, p. 7.
9   Ibid., pp. 135-6.

sins. The poets I have spoken about in these chapters are all well aware of
the mess these mistakes can make of our lives – Thomas Hardy in his sad
awkwardnesses[10] and susceptibilities, or Coleridge in the general mess of
his life, and above all they are reflected in the careful, layered language
of the poets of the English Renaissance and the seventeenth century –
Thomas Traherne and Sir Philip Sidney and their contemporaries. It is
with these poets that Geoffrey Hill truly comes alive and finds his deepest
inspiration, being on the whole impatient of modern poets, though one
himself. One of his best essays addresses 'The Absolute Reasonableness
of Robert Southwell',[11] the sixteenth century Catholic poet and priest
who was martyred in 1595 after three years of torture. Southwell was
canonized by the Roman Catholic Church in 1970. Like Sidney, he was
a master of classical rhetoric and infinitely careful language that allows
us, if we will give his poetry time, access beyond crude bombast or even
sophisticated generalization to the inner recesses of precise thought and
feeling, both human and divine. Geoffrey Hill describes Southwell's death
aptly – a death made holy by words well chosen:

> When he was brought out to endure 'the torments of a
> shameful death' Southwell could speak, with perfect calm
> and tact, in the idiom of his own *Epistle of Comfort*: 'I am
> come hither to play out the last act of this poor life'. Even at
> that moment he could retain his grasp on 'complexity' and
> yet speak with absolute simplicity. And it was such complex
> simplicity, I would finally claim, that enables this man of
> discipline to concede, in [his prose work] *Mary Magdalens
> Funeral Teares*, the 'wonderful alteration' of 'wildness' itself:
> 'Loue is not ruled with reason, but with loue'.[12]

But let us now turn to Hill's own poetry and begin by looking more
closely at the three lines of verse with which I began this chapter. Here
they are again:

> While all who attend to fiddle or to harp
> For betterment, flavour their decent mouths
> With gobbets of the sweetest sacrifice.

---

10 The word was used of Hardy by C.H. Sisson and quoted by Hill in *The Lords of
      Limit*, p. 135.
11 *The Lords of Limit*, pp. 19-37. Delivered as the Joseph Bard Memorial Lecture to
      the Royal Society of Literature, London, 17 May, 1979.
12 Ibid.. p. 37.

This is irony at its sharpest, reminiscent of the young T.S. Eliot in 'The Love Song of J. Alfred Prufrock', but harder and less implicit. Hill is expressing his impatience with hypocrisy in the church, among other things. It is about those people 'who attend' – attend what, church on Sunday morning? – 'to fiddle or to harp for betterment' – to get on, secure some form of advancement even. Hill never wastes words, and he makes them work hard. We play our instruments in church, tune our harps, but we are also fiddling about, harping on about things, 'for betterment'. Hill loves irony: we attend to make ourselves better – church-going is, after all, such an *improving* event. . . . Then there is the hardest cut of all – when we receive the sacrament itself, (each word in the poem is barbed), flavouring our oh-so-decent mouths – there are no nasty people here – with gobbets (the word almost drips with the blood – of Christ) of the sweetest sacrifice. Gobbets can, of course, be used also of words themselves, fragments of language or text taken out of context, usually for examination purposes. That puts us in our place (tending towards the sanctimonious as we so often are). But at the same time Geoffrey Hill's second wife was an ordained Anglican priest and one of his closest friends a senior Anglican bishop, and a deeply holy man – in those days you could be both at the same time.

In Hill's world, as in the *Book of Common Prayer*, words bite. I like that image, once suggested to me by the poet and Anglican priest David Scott, and that is why I use it a great deal. Words, used correctly, can uncover all hypocrisy and they allow no easy conclusions. Hill is capable, like Thomas Hardy, of writing the most beautiful of lyrics, but his preferred medium is the harsh phrase, the stumble out of and into meaning or, perhaps, inconclusiveness. There is a beautiful little poem in his first published book of verse, *For the Unfallen* (1959), entitled 'In Memory of Jane Fraser'. It reminds me of Wordsworth's celebrated Lucy poems, and I loved it when I first read it:

> When snow like sheep lay in the fold
> And winds went begging at each door,
> And the far hills were blue with cold,
> And a cold shroud lay on the moor,
> She kept the siege. . .[13]

---

13 Geoffrey Hill, *For the Unfallen: Poems* 1952-1958 (London: André Deutsch, 1959), p. 23.

It is everything that a lyric poem should be, with a lovely lilting rhythm and sharp images. I was, then, rather taken aback when I read in a later collection of Hill's poetry, published nine years later in 1968 and entitled *King Log*, these words:

> 'In Memory of Jane Fraser' was included in my first book *For the Unfallen*, which is now out of print. I dislike the poem very much and the publication of this amended version may be regarded as a necessary penitential exercise.[14]

The new version of the poem is subtitled 'An Attempted Reparation', and when I first read it and compared it with the original (which I had liked so much I had learnt it by heart) I could not for the life of me find any differences. Not a word was omitted or added. And then I noticed the punctuation. I had not read carefully enough, which is always fatal when reading Hill's poetry and prose. Apart from the necessary full stops all the commas had been omitted in the revised version. That was all. But this changes the rhythm and then the phrasing alters and it simply does not read so mellifluously or smoothly. Hill, of course, is chiding my Romantic spirit, making the poem harder to read, less reassuring – rather like a piece of music played at a constant and mechanical speed and volume level, true to the notes but without the tone or feeling, the pauses or the phrasing.

I came to realise that this was touching something at the very heart of this verse. It is not in any sense that Hill's poetry is 'mechanical', indeed, far from it, but he is not a lyric poet like Hardy (though he is perfectly capable of being so) – and he works phrase by phrase, more often in contradiction, and forcing each word to speak for itself. It is always hard work reading his poetry as it chides us for our lazy inattention to words and the structure of phrases, and chides our tendency, not least in our religious sensibilities, to fall into the seductions of graceful, easy patterns that mask true meaning, or simplifications which kill the very life and liveliness of words.

Since 2013 we have been able to read through the whole sequence of Hill's published poetry from *For the Unfallen* in 1959 to *The Daybooks* of 2007-2012, in one magnificent volume edited by Kenneth Haynes and entitled *Broken Hierarchies: Poems 1952-2012*. Religion and theology tend to be more overt, closer to the surface in the earlier pieces such as *Tenebrae* (1978) and *The Mystery of the Charity of Charles Péguy* (1983).

14 Geoffrey Hill, *King Log* (London: André Deutsch, 1968), p. 70.

And so I will come back in a moment to this earlier poetry, which actually I admit I prefer, it being more distanced and with less of the testiness and even bitterness of age, less of a tendency to the monologue. But first just a few more remarks on Hill's prose writings, focusing this time particularly on the book of his 1986 Clark Lectures, *The Enemy's Country: Words, Contexture, and other Circumstances of Language* (1991). Actually it is sometimes very difficult to distinguish his prose from his verse, each with a strange, complex beauty that is never easy to unveil.

Hill would probably never have made it as far as a professor in a university today. As I have remarked, he published only two fairly short books of literary essays, apart from his, admittedly fairly extensive, poetry and one English version of Henrik Ibsen's play *Brand*. It is not much in quantity, but anyone who tries to read *The Enemy's Country* quickly realises that every sentence is a challenge and a jewel and, as always with Hill, every word demands our total attention. After reading its just over one hundred pages you are left exhausted, mentally and spiritually. Most of the book, except one essay on the poet Ezra Pound, is, you will not now be surprised to hear, about seventeenth century writers. Here is a good example of his writing on the poet and priest John Donne. Hill reminds us that in Donne's *Essayes in Divinity* (he assumes, of course, that we will have read them!), Donne coins the term 'meta-theology' to suggest 'a profounder theology than that recognized by divines'. As a professor of literature and theology I should, of course, have known all about that. Poetry is often better at theology than theology itself – it is a *meta-theology*. So we move on to Donne's poetry itself in a typical Hill sentence, one poet responding to another:

> The knotty riddling of Donne's verse and prose moves from, and through, rhetorical bravado and 'alarums' (he himself enters that caveat) to an engagement with meta-poetics, a profounder poetry than that recognized by conventional instructors in rhetoric and conduct.[15]

Here is a double move. In poetry, carrying with it theology, we move into a meta-poetics that stands beside and outside convention. The orthodox theologian is, or should be, by now, beginning to feel uncomfortable and somewhat displaced. Poetry takes theology outside itself into the contexture of paradox – Hill uses Donne's familiar line of

---

15   Geoffrey Hill, *In the Enemy's Country* (Oxford: The Clarendon Press, 1991), p. 59.

verse, 'When thou hast done, thou hast not done,'[16] with its pun on the poet's own name. Here is his comment, employing words from Donne's own prose:[17]

> There is none the less an irreducible paradox or oxymoron in the mundane constitution, and the literary paradox is a formal submission that 'things' are so: 'they have been written in an age when anything is strong enough to overthrow [truth].'[18]

That last word, 'truth', is written in square brackets, the two poets, Donne and Hill addressing us in one voice. We are meant to struggle with this, and we do. If we take enough care it makes perfectly good sense, but on the whole, I fear, we tend to be careless with language and do not make enough effort, or take enough time, to understand. We think that language should do the work for us and we forget that even in the everyday use of words, what Hill calls the 'mundane constitution', there lies unexplored paradoxes and wonders – rather as Wordsworth saw in the daffodils beside Ullswater, or Jesus saw in the Galilean farmer sowing seed. Poetry or literature, that thrives on paradoxes, merely then reminds us that things are indeed as they are – but they show us a complex reality as we generally fail to notice it because we cannot stand aside from it with the insight of a *meta*-poetry or a *meta*-theology. We prefer to avoid the direct challenge in the language, the question – 'what do *you* think?' And such an obvious recognition of and confrontation with the real is essential in an age – like Donne's and perhaps even more like our own – when the truth, with all its riddles and delicacy, is liable to be overthrown by any chance wind that blows. In short, the poet is the guardian of our times in lapidary words that can resist the chances and changes of this fleeting life.

Later in *The Enemy Country* Hill suggests that the function of art is simply to remind us that *things are so* – often even against the power of what we sometimes loosely call 'common sense'. He recalls, as I did in the earlier chapter on Thomas Hardy, those lines of Hardy who as an old, doubting man in his poem 'The Oxen' creeps back on Christmas

---

16 John Donne, 'A Hymn to God the Father', *The Complete English Poems*, ed. by A.J. Smith (Harmonsworth: Penguin, 1971), p. 348.

17 John Donne, *Selected Prose*. Chosen by E. Simpson (Oxford: Oxford University Press, 1967), p. 111.

18 *In the Enemy's Country*, p. 59.

Eve to the stable of the incarnation with the poignant (that word is Hill's, not mine) 'hoping it might be so', a phrase that is 'pitched against [the] *affects* of common sense'.[19] True religion and true poetry have always suspected the simplifications of common sense, a form of 'sense' which we, I fear, tend to overvalue. The prophets of the Hebrew Bible, with whom Hill bears some resemblance both in appearance and in manner, did not have much common sense, and nor did Jesus on the cross. Hill puts me in mind, somehow, of the intrepid explorer Gertrude Bell's wonderful description of the prophets of old whose descendants still lurk in the remote desert places of the Holy Land, 'a race of starved and gaunt ascetics, clinging to a tradition of piety that common sense has found it hard to discredit'.[20] But Hill goes back to the words of Hardy's poem of old age – words that admit that *knowing* the Christmas stable is nonsense, but still *hoping* it *might* not be. If we are honest, can we say much more? And perhaps it is enough, it *does*, using the words written for Christmas of another poet, W.H. Auden, for the time being.

Hill's prose is not to be trifled with. And no more is the poetry, which can be even more unforgiving of literary carelessness. It requires our persistence, borne and accompanied with the words from Psalm 90: 14 that appear on the dedication page of *Broken Hierarchies*: 'O satisfy us early with thy mercy; that we may rejoice and be glad all our days'.

And so to the poem of Geoffrey Hill that is, perhaps, my favourite, if such a description can be appropriate for so dark a piece. Perhaps haunting would be a better word than dark. It is entitled 'Canticle for Good Friday', written in 1956 when Hill was a young man of just twenty-four, and published in his first collection of poems. Here it is in full:

> The cross staggered him. At the cliff-top
> Thomas, beneath its burden, stood
> While the dulled wood
> Spat on the stones each drop
> Of deliberate blood.
>
> A clamping, cold-figured day
> Thomas (not transfigured) stamped, crouched,

---

19 Ibid., p. 86.
20 Gertrude Bell, *The Desert and the Sown* [1907] (New York: Cooper Square Press, 2001), p. 10.

Watched
Smelt vinegar and blood. He,
As yet unsearched, unscratched,

And suffered to remain
At such near distance
(A slight miracle might cleanse
His brain
Of all attachments, claw-roots of sense)

In unaccountable darkness moved away
The strange flesh untouched, carrion-substance
Of staunchest love, choicest defiance,
Creation's issue congealing (and one woman's).[21]

Let us look at the poem and its careful language more closely. The first word of the title initiates an ironic tone – it is a 'canticle' or song for Good Friday, a liturgical utterance, and it is seen from the perspective of Doubting Thomas, an ordinary man, like us, 'not transfigured', a disciple who was not present at Jesus' transfiguration before the final journey to Jerusalem. Hill focuses on the darkest moment of the Passion narrative, on Christ on the cross, and every word, every phrase makes its demands, holds us back, challenges us, perplexes and assaults our mind and senses. Thomas staggers and is 'staggered' as the cross, under whose shadow he stands, becomes his burden. Hill employs the full rhetorical devices of poetry – at the end of the first stanza, the alliteration of spat/stones; drop/ deliberate – almost physically enacts the flow of blood, the image and alliteration looking back in English poetry as far as the Old English poem *The Dream of the Rood* from perhaps as early as the eighth century.[22] (I am reminded also of Isaac Watt's tremendous Passiontide hymn, 'When I survey the wondrous cross', in which we are bidden to *see* the blood flowing down Christ's body as love and sorrow.)

As we have noted, Hill is very precise, economical not only with words but with his punctuation. He shows us how to measure the poem and its rhythm in a poem of phrases that hold back their sense and meaning even as they seem to offer them. The second stanza begins again with alliterative precision on the coldness of Good Friday, its first two lines

---

21 Geoffrey Hill, *For the Unfallen*, p. 39.
22 *The Dream of the Rood* is found, in three parts in the tenth century Vercelli Book. Lines from it are also inscribed on the eighth century Ruthwell Cross in Dumfriesshire.

employing one of Hill's favourite rhetorical devices in the paranomasia of cold-figured/transfigured. And it is Thomas that we see and watch (just as in the *Stabat Mater* we see and watch the Virgin Mary) – not the figure on the cross – in four expressive verbs: stamped, crouched, watched, smelt. Hill is relentless in holding us to the moment. Then we move on in anticipation to the Thomas of the resurrection appearance of Christ when he demanded to feel the wounds of the Passion before he would believe (John 20: 24-29). But even now he is still the figure who is not yet tested – unsearched, unscratched, and at a distance though so painfully close.

Here Thomas is the one who is suffered, and who suffers – bound to the cross yet still distant, wanting a slight miracle that will get him away from all this unutterable pain. But his brain remains attached, working. The verse becomes yet more impenetrable, and in the final stanza, word by agonizing word, I am reminded, perhaps, of W.B. Yeats' poem 'The Second Coming', with its mysterious beast slouching towards Bethlehem to be born. The figure on the cross is dead, a corpse and food for the crows – carrion sustenance – yet still the strange flesh remains untouched by Thomas ('Except I see . . . and thrust my hand into his side, I will not believe', John 20: 25), described in those strange words: 'staunchest love, choicest defiance'. And then there is the final, awful line about the issue of all creation, first-born (Christ is the second Adam, the first child of his mother), congealing in cold blood, and the abrupt shift from the universal to the painful particular, remembered almost as an afterthought in brackets in the last words of the poem – '(and one woman's)'. Jesus was, after all, a man, the son of one woman, Mary, who was also present at the crucifixion, though not mentioned here.

Beyond the poetry there is a meta-poetry, and beyond the meta-poetry there is a meta-theology. Always beyond. We are, or we should be, working hard, suffering to understand. This calls to and revises our smoothed-out theology, both the known and the subconscious, unraveling the neat packaging with which we have bound our thoughts, the feelings and the spirituality of Good Friday. As readers we are dissected. Like Thomas, beneath the burden of the cross, we stand, as it were, on a cliff-top, teetering on the edge between belief and unbelief, uncertain, fearful (if we are honest), demanding to see and touch so that, by a miracle that never comes, we might *know*. How we long to know. Such is our song for Good Friday. Theology, or rather meta-theology, threads its way through most of Hill's early poems, even in their titles: 'God's Little Mountain', 'Holy Thursday', 'Picture of a Nativity', 'Little Apocalypse'. They are interwoven with strange, liturgical and demanding learning – Hill expects us to know it all and he must have been a hard teacher – resisting conclusion. The fashion in modern theology, and certainly in modern liturgical writing, is for clarity and simplicity; simplicity of language and therefore of thought. We are not satisfied until the language is clear and plain enough for us to understand – but that is not enough for the true poet. Hill makes his words complex, rich, allusive, hard – and leads us into world of meta-theology that we seldom dare, or even would wish, to visit. But the poet knows the power of such words, the guardians of our faith, the beginnings of a grammar of assent, and of truth itself, if we will listen, within which our comprehension may rest – words as the lords of limit, as Hill calls them, drawing upon the verse of his fellow poet W.H. Auden.[23]

One more verse from the early poetry before we move briefly into the more angry world of Hill's later work. I especially love one stanza from the poem 'In Piam Memoriam'. It describes the image of the saint on a stained glass window, a saint 'created purely from glass':

> In the sun lily-and-gold-coloured,
> Filtering the cruder light, he has endured,
> A feature for our regard; and will keep;
> Of worldly purity the stained archetype.[24]

As always the image is delicately drawn in words as the cruder light of the outside day is filtered and transformed by the saint in glass himself. But it is the last line that counts most: 'Of worldly purity the stained archetype'. Like a seventeenth century metaphysical poet Hill always makes language work on more than one level at once. It takes a moment before we respond fully to those last two words, 'stained archetype'. This is, after all, a piece of *stained* glass from which the saint has been 'created *purely*'. But we have also read it another way – being creatures, like even the saints themselves, of the human stain – and the archetype is an image, at once stained and unblemished: an image, in sight and word, of salvation.

---

23 Hill takes this phrase, the title of his first book of essays, from his fellow poet W.H. Auden, 'O Lords of Limit, training dark and light'. 'The Watchers', *Collected Shorter Poems 1927-1957* (London: Faber, 1966), p. 52. It appears more than once in Hill's own verse.

24 *For the Unfallen*, p. 58.

Hill once quoted some words of Ezra Pound, another poet who meant much to him: 'You cannot call a man an artist until he has shown himself capable of reticence and restraint, until he shows himself in some degree master of the forces which beat upon him.'[25] We do not choose our place in the world but we are necessarily an 'inextricable part' of the circumstances under which we exist. But this is no mere fatalism, and the poet must at the same time be the master, or, may be, mistress, enduring all with restraint, not anger (one thinks of Job), and him – or herself mastering inevitabilities by the sheer force of living words. Yet this is never easy, never relaxed, as we have seen. Hill dislikes intensely the easy option and the reassuring, easy lyric. The title of *The Enemy's Country* is drawn from the 'Epistle Dedicatorie' of Thomas Nash and William Davenant's work *Strange News of the Intercepting Certain Letters* (1592), and more fully reads, 'This is your enemies' country which they took in the small hours an age before you woke.'[26] We are, in short, in a country that has been invaded while we slept unawares, and into this land words must now boldly enter, wholly alert, if we are to survive. Hill writes of how integrity so easily falls 'into the merely sincere': and 'beauty – against the grain of the argument – remains "a brief gasp between one cliché and another".'[27] I love that gasp of astonishment between clichés as beauty reveals itself against the grain of the argument – a deeply religious, finally unstated moment. And the withering phrase 'merely sincere' summarises a persistent theme of Hill's later poetry – his hatred of false or assumed piety in church. One poem in *A Treatise of Civil Power* (2007) has the biting, cutting lines:

> Let's all shore up
> half-decent lives this Lent, *happy and holy.*
> Two or three people I would call saints
> without lust for sincerity which
> Marcel describes,
> *An exaltation in one's negative*
> *powers.*[28]

25 *The Enemy's Country*, p. 5. The words are from Ezra Pound, *Patria Mia* (Chicago: R.F. Seymour, 1950), p. 47.
26 Quoted as a frontispiece to *The Enemy's Country*.
27 *The Enemy's Country*, p. 102.
28 *Broken Heirarchies*, p. 584.

To put this more crudely, Hill has no time for the holier-than-thou people, those with a lust for sincerity, the unctuously self-deprecating Christians.

As Hill developed as a poet from the astonishing early poems of *For The Unfallen*, theology and religious themes, usually in the context of invectives against the corruption of the church, insistently continue to haunt his work. After the poems of *King Log* (1968), in *Mercian Hymns*, *Tenebrae*, *The Mystery of the Charity of Charles Péguy* and *Canaan*, Hill persistently explores a fallen world, almost overwhelmed with the violence perpetrated by human beings on one another. I confess that, for me, as the rage and anger of old age begin to sound more loudly in the poetry his verse loses something of the riddling subtleties of his early work, though the power of words, composed almost as monologues, continues to be felt. The critic Harold Bloom has written of Hill as the heir of William Blake and D.H. Lawrence, his language the instrument of the poet-prophet (though if Blake, in his *Memorable Fancy*, dines with Isaiah and Ezekiel, one imagines Hill dining only with the grim Jeremiah[29]) as he inveighs against the horrors of war and the Holocaust, against religious institutions and private religiosity, and against the unbearable tensions between public and private life. In his fairly late book-length poem *The Triumph of Love* (1998), Hill explores the theme of forgiveness – or, as he prefers to describe it, the 'slow haul to forgive'.

Amidst endless biblical references (above all from the apocalyptic writings in the Book of Daniel), Hill begins ('last things first') with a reflection on the violence and dishonesty of the twentieth century from Neville Chamberlain's 'compliant vanity' to the horrors of Dunkirk and the ash pits of the Holocaust – and then the 'slow haul to forgive them'.[30] All this is played out, ironically, against the treasured background of the Authorized Version, which has, after all, 'seen better days' (as always in more ways than one) – nation against nation in imagined peace and impending war, Hill always the scrupulous poet:

> a telling figure out of rhetoric,
> epanalepsis, the same word first and last.[31]

---

29 William Blake, *The Marriage of Heaven and Hell* [1790-93], 'A Memorable Fancy', in *Complete Writings*, ed. by Geoffrey Keynes (Oxford: Oxford University Press, 1972), p. 153.

30 Geoffrey Hill, *The Triumph of Love: A Poem* (Harmondsworth: Penguin, 1999), X, p. 4.

31 Ibid.

Hill, adopting (in his case with some natural authority) the tone of the curmudgeonly old man, gives himself license to say precisely what he thinks, though he is under no delusions about himself and he does not mince words about himself:

> Shameless old man, bent on committing
> more public nuisance. Incontinent
> fury wetting the air. Impotently
> bereft satire. Charged with erudition,
> put up by the defence to be
> his own accuser.[32]

Hill, the word-smith, remains rooted in the deliberate double meanings that still bite and bite back: that '*charged* with erudition' – an energy but also an accusation and a summons felt by every true intellectual in an age of dangerously, outrageously trumped up simplifications, and yet he is fully charged – and full well knows the problem. Hill is the impotent saviour of words that get carelessly and dangerously muddled and muddied. He detests the commoner (he is, at last, a Cambridge don after all) who does not care what he or she says, but the moment of revelation slips between the meanings, for he, as a poet, will say what he will say. Hill's poetry is unforgiving to the careless reader, forceful upon the letter or syllable missed out or misread, even as he seeks forgiveness:

> For wordly, read worldly; for equity, inequity
> for religious read religiose; for distinction
> detestation. Take accessible to mean
> acceptable, accommodating, openly servile.
> *Is that right, Missis, or is that right?* I don't
> Care what I say, do I?[33]

In this poem of love Hill charges with rapier words all cruelties, dishonesties and hypocrisy. 'For iconic priesthood, read worldly pique and ambition'.[34] And yet there are saintly bishops also in this poem. At the beginning I referred to Hill's old friend Bishop Peter Walker, of Dorchester and Ely (and my ordaining bishop). Peter is mentioned, without name and with some bitterness as regards today's world, in *The Triumph of Love* in a reference to the sinking of HMS Broadwater

---

32 Ibid., XXXVII, p. 19.
33 Ibid., XL, pp. 20-1.
34 Ibid., XLI, p. 21.

during the Second World War, the convoy escort on which Walker, as a
young wartime naval rating should have been serving, but he was away
on shore leave. It is a passage that asks, without pity, whether the society
of today warrants or is even worth such sacrifice of life:

> By what right did . . .
> the trapped below-decks watch
> of Peter's clangerous old destroyer-escort,
> serve to enfranchise these strange children
> pitiless in their ignorance and contempt?[35]

Hill is thinking here of a haunting sermon that Peter Walker once
preached in Brasenose College chapel in Oxford where the phrase,
'with all the watch below' resounds repeatedly through words spoken
regarding the sinking of the ship on which he should have been serving.

As always, as from the very beginning in his poetry, Geoffrey Hill
demands much of his reader, and he expects us to be as educated
in literature as he is in what he knows to be a woefully ill-educated
age – ill-educated in the business of the humanities in spite of all our
resources. In *The Triumph of Love* it is the Bible that haunts every page,
but also Shakespeare (you know, after all, your *Measure for Measure*),
Milton, Traherne (whom we now understand better. 'I/am an old man,
a child, the horizon/is Traherne's country', writes Hill[36]), or Cocteau
(less well known), the music of Bartók (dying in New York), Eugenio
Montale (who? You don't know? After all he did win the Nobel Prize for
Literature in 1975), D.H. Lawrence (ah, that's better). I could go on . . ..

So what is all this about? Are these just the dust heaps of our
civilization being blown backwards into history like Paul Klee's *Angelus
Novus* in Walter Benjamin's notable Thesis IX on the Philosophy of
History?[37] Hill's point is that now we don't even care – we have given up,
merely shaking our heads at the wrecks of time and the sins of our age.
At the end of the poem, he sees himself beginning to become confused,
even senile, still writing (people have already half-forgotten him) in a
hopeless moment of hope, perhaps?

> Obstinate old man – *senex*
> *sapiens*, it is not. Is he still
> writing? What is he writing now? He

---

35 Ibid., LXXVII, p. 40.
36 Ibid., CXXI, p. 64.
37 Walter Benjamin, *Illuminations*. Trans. Harry Zohn (London: Fontana Press, 1973), p. 249.

> has just written: I find it hard
> to forgive myself. We are immortal. Where
> was I? –[38]

But what are poems for, he asks? 'They are to console us', if we give them time and attention, though it may be '*a sad and angry consolation*'. At the end of this long poem, in a kaleidoscope of references from Ezra Pound, John Ruskin's *Fors Clavigera*, William Tyndale whose 'unshowy diligence' (that phrase captures him perfectly) gave us the foundations of the English King James Bible, and the Italian poet Torquato Tasso – two notes sound above all the others: they are heard from St Augustine's great work *The City of God*, and St Paul's great song of God's self-emptying in to the world in his Letter to the Philippians, the Kenotic Hymn – '*God . . . made himself of no reputation . . . took/the shape of a servant*.'[39]

Although *The Triumph of Love* is an extraordinary achievement, I find it, finally, less satisfying than Hill's earlier verse – it is a bit too self-conscious, bordering even perhaps on the self-pitying at times. Often in the later poetry there is a sense of being slightly forced or strained, as when he presents himself in *The Daybooks*:

> Illiterate I would blaze myself the un-
> tutored elect of language: it's that strong –
> Stronger almost than Keats with his mute urn -[40]

And so, in conclusion, let me return to the book with which I began, *King Log* (1968), in which Hill's cryptic, mythic imagination is nearly consistently at its best. There are poems on violence, poems on poems and poets, and one on love, entitled 'Annunications, (2)':

> O Love, subject of the mere diurnal grind,
> Forever being pledged to be redeemed,
> Expose yourself for charity; be assured
> The body is but husk and excrement.
> Enter these deaths according to the law,
> O visited women, possessed sons! Foreign lusts
> Infringe our restraints; the changeable
> Soldiery have their goings-out and comings-in

---

38 *The Triumph of Love*, CXLIX, p. 82.
39 Ibid., CXLVI, p. 80.
40 *Broken Hierarchies*, p. 695.

Dying in abundance. Choicest beasts
Suffuse the gutters with their colourful blood.
Our God scatters corruption. Priests, martyrs,
Parade to this imperious theme: 'O Love,
You know what pains succeed; be vigilant; strive
To recognize the damned among your friends.'[41]

Journeying with Hill is, as we have seen, never comfortable. There are moments of recognition and reprieve, echoes of the familiar, then a shocking image of sacrifice, and they do not seem quite to hold together. And, in the end, there is always an unease, or perhaps better a provocation to thought and reflection. So let us end this chapter, with those last lines to Love, on the theme of priests and martyrs. What are pains that succeed? The pains of the crucifixion, or of martyrdom – dying that others might live? Pain that is useful? Love must be vigilant – to do what? 'To recognize the damned among your friends.' That is a hard line. Is this just harsh realism – that even in the company of love there are those who are not what they seem to be? Love, beware.

Geoffrey Hill is a troubling poet. I would have liked to set him beside a more widely known poet of the twentieth century, W.H. Auden, whose relationship with the Church of England was, in some ways, similar, but a poet, finally, of a far more (I hesitate to use the phrase) middle class, bourgeois bearing. Hill, in my view, is one of the greatest religious poets writing in English of the twentieth century. I rate him, finally, above T.S. Eliot, though he is far less well known and less read, perhaps because he is more difficult and less hospitable to the cultured reader. For Eliot has a tendency to adopt a pose even in his greatest works like *The Four Quartets*, and this Hill never does. It is Hill's relentless honesty that I most deeply admire. Nothing for him is ever simple, and words therefore must be precise, as sharp as razors – and they can cut us to the quick. Hill is never easy company – but he is always worth the time spent with him, and even when we feel we do not understand what he is saying, in prose or verse, if you make the effort, you will always come away with the sense that something is different, that something new has happened. It is, perhaps, the gift of poetry, a healing gift, an act of atonement, the gift of the Word.

---

41 *King Log*, p. 15.

7.
The Pastoral Tradition in English Poetry

This final chapter will be a little different from those which precede it, for it will not focus upon one poet, but upon a tradition of poetry – that which I call the 'pastoral'. Exactly thirty years ago, in 1988, my old friend Professor Jim Barcus of Baylor University, Texas, invited me to write an article for the journal *Christianity and Literature*, of which he was then the editor, on religious poetry in English. The result was a piece entitled 'Two or Three Gathered in His Name: Reflections on the English Pastoral Tradition in Religious Poetry'[1] and what I will say here differs relatively little from that earlier essay though, inevitably, there will be some additions and expansions. But basically my love affair with poetry continues unchanged, though the context is different – and more of that later.

Much more recently, in 2007, I edited an essay by the remarkable Anglican priest and contemporary poet, David Scott, similarly entitled 'Pastoral Tradition in Religious Poetry' for *The Oxford Handbook of English Literature and Theology*.[2] Scott defines this

---

1   *Christianity and Literature*, Vol. XXXVIII, No. 1 (Fall, 1988) 19-32.
2   Andrew Hass, David Jasper and Elisabeth Jay, Eds, *The Oxford Handbook of English Literature and Theology* (Oxford: Oxford University Press, 2007), pp. 726-41.

tradition much better and more accurately than I did, as growing out of the ministry of the (largely Anglican and Church of England) church and rooted in the parish, its community and what Scott calls 'a pastoral consciousness'[3] in Christian ministry. This is a tradition that goes back at least to the fourteenth century and probably much earlier than that, and still continues today despite all assaults of 'digital' or 'entrepreneurial' mission or business models and strategic plans in the hierarchy of the church. A scattered group calling itself 'The Poetry Church: an Inclusive Congregation' first published its regular collections of poems many years ago under the editorship of an Anglican priest, the late John Waddington-Feather, and it continues to this day. It may not always publish great poetry but it has a particular voice that is, perhaps, important and not heard enough. I am writing this in the context of an article written recently, apparently entirely without irony, in the *Guardian* newspaper by Andrew Brown extolling the style of the current Archbishop of Canterbury as he 'combines energy, ruthlessness and a determination to get the church moving, through a mixture of public theatricality and arm-twisting behind the scenes.'[4] However that may be true or not, there can certainly be no future in such a church for it will have lost its soul in its pursuit of efficiency, and lost also its necessary humility and perhaps hiddenness.

The pastoral tradition in poetry, on the other hand, has its foundations not in business-like ruthlessness but in the liturgy and prayers of the church, and above all, in the Church of England and the *Book of Common Prayer*. The 1662 office of Evening Prayer concludes with what we know as 'A Prayer of Saint Chrysostom':

> Almighty God, who hast given us grace at this time with one accord to make our common supplications unto thee: and dost promise that when two or three are gathered in they Name thou wilt grant their requests.[5]

We begin in simplicity and utter humility, even if just in twos or threes. But this tradition in poetry also takes its tone from the

---

3   Ibid., p. 726.

4   Andrew Brown, 'With piety and steel, Welby has the church in his firmest grip', *The Guardian* (Journal), Friday, 16 February 2018, pp. 1-2.

5   *The Book of Common Prayer: The Texts of 1549, 1559, and 1662*, ed. by Brian Cummings (Oxford: Oxford University Press, 2011), p. 257.

Prayer Book Ordinal – that is the manner of making, ordaining and consecrating deacons, priests and bishops. The priest's ministry is defined as above all that of the shepherd, 'to seek for Christ's sheep that are dispersed abroad, and for his children who are in the midst of this naughty world, that they may be saved through Christ forever'. Such a pastoral ministry can never be easy or obvious, for it will experience the pain of failure and inadequacy, and in it 'the will and ability is given of God alone'.[6] One of the key words that recur in the poetry of the pastoral tradition is 'uselessness' – that sense of waste which perhaps must inevitably be so much part of a ministry which serves not itself but God. It is nothing new. In the seventeenth century, the pious priest and poet George Herbert wrote at the end of his Sunday labours, having exhausted himself and done his best:

> I ranne; but all I brought was fome.
>
>   Thy diet, care, and cost
> Do end in bubbles, balls of winde;
>   Of winde to thee whom I have crost,
> But balls of wilde-fire to my troubled minde.[7]

But in spite of all this the pastoral tradition in English poetry, its piety and tone, are rooted in a ministry of the church that has its heart in loving care and its basis in Scripture and the liturgy. By no means all of its poets are Anglican and certainly not all are ordained. As we might expect in such a traditionally patriarchal church there are relatively few voices of women, but they are present (as we have seen in the Countess of Pembroke and there are others later, as we shall see in a moment) and they are important. The *Prayer Book* psalms of Miles Coverdale are everywhere present in this poetic tradition within Anglicanism, not surprisingly as they are said morning and evening each day in the offices, and largely from them in the seventeenth century a tradition of Anglican piety grew in which the line dividing poetry from prose was almost imperceptible – as in the prayers, the *Preces Privatae*, of Bishop Lancelot Andrewes (a friend of George Herbert), first translated into English in 1630 and then in 1840 by John Henry Newman, and the haunting prose of Bishop Jeremy Taylor. It is a tradition continued in our own time in the writings and poetry of Archbishop Rowan

---

6   Ibid., p. 636.
7   George Herbert, 'Even-song', *The English Poems*, ed. by Helen Wilcox (Cambridge: Cambridge University Press, 2007), p. 231.

Williams (actually a Welshman and therefore far from alone amongst poets), a tradition of what Williams calls, in a slightly different tone, 'Anglican identities'.[8]

But we must begin much earlier than the seventeenth century. One of my most treasured books is F.N. Robinson's edition of *The Works of Geoffrey Chaucer*, given to me by my father in 1968 when I was still at school. Readers of England's first great national poet, writing in the fourteenth century, quickly become acquainted with the corruptions of the various churchmen of *The Canterbury Tales* – the Pardoner, or the wanton and merry Friar - but tend to spend less time with the saintly poor Parson of the town. He sets a pattern for parochial pastoral ministry, being learned, living as he teaches, faithfully visiting his flock, never tempted by the snares of London and a man, we may say, of 'cleanness' (an important quality in Middle English). Two things in particular strike me about this medieval parson: first, there is his persistence as a character in both literature and the life of the church up to the present day, and he remains even now a good model for any ordinand beginning a new ministry. In him Chaucer is perfectly well aware of the seductions of the capital city and of preferment in the church. Some things never change. Second, and it is not unrelated, this ministry is both at the very heart of the church's life, and, at the same time, institutionally on its edge. The Parson's closest contemporary pastoral colleagues in literature, in some ways, are to be found in Lollard texts – Lollards being the followers of the fourteenth century Oxford scholar and priest John Wycliffe and in many ways the precursors of the Reformation – in works like *Jack Upland* or the apocryphal *Plowman's Tale*, both probably written in the early fifteenth century.[9] Lollards lived on the very edge of the church, or indeed beyond it, and sometimes they paid the ultimate price for that.

But Chaucer sums up his Parson and his qualities:

> A bettre preest I trowe that nowher noon ys.
> He waited after no pompe and reverence,
> Ne maked him a spiced conscience,
> But Cristes lore and his apostles twelve
> He taught, but first he folwed it hymselve.[10]

---

8   Rowan Williams, *Anglican Identities* (London: Darton, Longman and Todd, 2004).

9   *Jack Upland, Friar Daw's Reply and Upland's Rejoinder*, ed. by P.L. Heyworth (Oxford: Oxford University Press, 1968). *The Plowman's Tale*, in *Six Ecclesiastical Satires*, ed. by James Dean (Kalamazoo: Medieval Institute Publications, 1991).

10 *The General Prologue* to *The Canterbury Tales*, ll. 524-8. In, *The Works of*

The medieval Parson's reincarnation in the figure of the Revd George Herbert (1593-1633) finds him in the early seventeenth century, saturated in both his language and spirituality in the poetry and theology of the Anglican *Book of Common Prayer* and the English of William Tyndale's Bible translation. I have already written about this at length in my book *The Language of Liturgy* (2018) and I do not wish to repeat myself here. Let me say just two things about Herbert about whom so much has already been written – his intricacy and his ordinariness. Students of literature will generally begin with the poems of Herbert the 'metaphysical' poet, standing beside his fellow cleric John Donne as a master of intricate rhetoric and word-play. But although our prayers may indeed form the richness of, in Herbert's phrase, 'the Church's banquet', yet they may also be the finding of 'heaven in ordinary'.[11] There is nothing wrong in being ordinary or plain of speech. As the shepherd of his flock in the parish of Bemerton, near Salisbury, Herbert, once the famed and learned public orator at the University of Cambridge between 1619 and 1627, knew the human need for 'ordinariness', for adaption to the frailties and even simply the prosaic quality of everyday life. In his prose work, *A Priest to the Temple* (1632), a parson's handbook that is still of profound value today (perhaps, indeed, more so than ever), Herbert acknowledges that the country parson 'is generally sad', knowing the depth of sin by which God is disfigured. Yet instruction must also be seasoned with humour and 'mirth':

> Whereof he condescends to humane frailties both in himself and others, and intermingles some mirth in his discourses occasionally, according to the pulse of the hearer.[12]

The good parson both and at once stands aside from and yet is entirely one with his flock. The word 'condescends' has rather changed its meaning since Herbert's day. Today it is a somewhat unpleasant word, implying a looking down from an assumed great and superior height. But Herbert meant it literally – a parson should 'con-descend', come down and become one with his people. This, for the educated man, might be an occasion of some loneliness. And Herbert does properly 'condescend'

Geoffrey Chaucer, ed. by F.N. Robinson, 2nd edn. (London: Oxford University Press, 1957), p. 22.

11 George Herbert, 'Prayer (1)', *The English Poems*, p. 178.

12 George Herbert, *The Temple* and *A Priest to the Temple* (London: J.M. Dent, 1902), 'The Parson in Mirth', p. 267.

now and then in his writing of poetry. His version of Psalm 23 is quite different in style from most of his sacred verse. It was intended to be, and is still thus used today, a hymn in which, in the words of Donald Davie, 'he contrived a special rusticity so as to appeal to an unlettered congregation'.[13] It is simple but beautifully constructed, deeply pastoral:

> The God of love my shepherd is,
>   And he that doth me feed;
> While he is mine, and I am his,
>   What can I want or need?
>
> . . .
>
> Surely thy sweet and wondrous love
>   Shall measure all my days;
> And as it never shall remove,
>   So neither shall my praise.[14]

We should never despise the poetry of the hymn, instilling profound Christian theology in the clearest and simplest form and image.[15] Such pastoral wisdom is carried into the eighteenth century, and not only in the Anglican tradition.

The Congregational minister Isaac Watts (1674-1748) has, perhaps, the misfortune of being the butt of one of Lewis Carroll's best parodies ('How doth the little crocodile') of Watts' poem 'Against Idleness and Mischief' in *Divine Songs for Children* (1715):

> How doth the little busy bee
>   Improve each shining hour,
> And gather honey all the day
>   From every opening flower![16]

The original is entirely overwhelmed by the parody. But, like George Herbert, Watts was well aware of the needs and limitations of his flock, and sought to bring to them the treasures of the Psalms in hymns that are rooted in both scripture and the world around us. In his *A Short Essay Toward the Improvement of Psalmody* (1748), published in the year of his death, Watts admits that 'it was hard to restrain my verse

---

13 Donald Davie (Ed.) *The Psalms in English* (Harmondsworth: Penguin, 1996), p. 118.
14 Ibid., pp. 117-18.
15 See J.R. Watson, *Awake My Soul: Reflections on Thirty Hymns* (London: SPCK, 2005).
16 Michael R. Turner (Selected), *Parlour Poetry: A Hundred and One Improving Gems* (London: Michael Joseph, 1967), p. 38.

always within the bounds of my design; it was hard to sink every line to the level of a whole congregation, and yet to keep it above contempt.'[17]

It is a problem highlighted by poetic genius about which, I dare to suggest, we are less sensitive today in our pastoral care and teaching which can so often be unconsciously banal and over-simplified – perhaps sometimes condescending in the bad sense. At his best, Watts (and he was phenomenally successful both in his day and into the nineteenth century) gets it just right. His poem, 'A Prospect of Heaven Makes Death Easy', is still sung as a hymn in our churches. It combines biblical teaching that draws on the motif of the Pisgah Height from which the dying Moses saw the Promised Land of Canaan (Deuteronomy 34), with descriptions of the English countryside outside the windows of parish churches of the singing congregation – the countryside that Thomas Hardy, as a child, was to gaze out on in rural 'Mellstock' just over one hundred years later:[18]

> There is a land of pure delight
> Where saints immortal reign;
> Infinite day excludes the night,
> And pleasures banish pain.
>
> . . .
>
> Sweet fields beyond the swelling flood
> Stand dressed in living green:
> So to the Jews old Canaan stood,
> While Jordan rolled between.[19]

Like Herbert, Watts can bring together two worlds that are yet one – and he brings heaven to the very fields and lanes of his congregation's parish.

Towards the end of the eighteenth century, and returning to the Anglican tradition, the poet William Cowper collaborated with the evangelical clergyman the Revd John Newton to produce the *Olney Hymns* (1779), from the village of Olney in Buckinghamshire near Bedford, England. The origin of such familiar hymns as 'Glorious things of thee are spoken' and 'God moves in a mysterious way', the

---

17 Quoted in Donald Davie, *A Gathered Church: The Literature of the English Dissenting Interest, 1700-1930* (London: Routledge & Kegan Paul, 1978), p. 24.

18 In 'Afternoon Service at Mellstock (*circa* 1850)'.

19 Donald Davie (Ed.) *The New Oxford Book of Christian Verse* (Oxford: Oxford University Press, 1981), p. 149.

Olney Hymns, in John Newton's Preface, provide an opportunity for a humble acknowledgement of Watts' pastoral wisdom in pursuing in verse what we might call the 'art of sinking':[20]

> The late Dr. Watts . . . might, as a poet, have a right to say, that it cost him some labour to restrain his fire, and to accommodate himself to the capacities of common readers. But it would not become me to make such a declaration. It behoved me to do my best. But though I would not offend readers of taste by a wilful coarseness, and negligence, I do not write professedly for them. If the Lord whom I serve, has been pleased to favor me with that mediocrity of talent, which may qualify me for usefulness to the weak and poor of his flock, without quite disgusting persons of superior discernment, I have reason to be satisfied.[21]

Once again, the problem is not unfamiliar today.

In his great poem *The Task* (1785), Cowper seems to revisit once more the character of Chaucer's ancient Parson. Being a true pastor to the flock is not simply a matter of fine words, but of deeds, the manner of life and a true heart: preaching may be easy as words can be manipulated, but what of the honesty of the heart?

>   The voice
>   Is but an instrument on which the priest
>   May play what tune he pleases. In the deed,
>   The unequivocal authentic deed,
>   We find sound argument, we read the heart.[22]

Such inward integrity lies at the very centre of this pastoral tradition in poetry. As we move into the nineteenth century, William Wordsworth drew upon the ministry of the remarkable Anglican clergyman the Revd Robert Walker[23] who was incumbent of Holy Trinity, Seathwaite from 1736 until his death in 1802 at the age of ninety-two, and was popularly known as 'Wonderful Walker'. In the sonnet 'Seathwaite

---

20 The phrase is used by Alexander Pope and the Scriblerus Club in the eighteenth century.

21 John Newton, Preface to *Olney Hymns* [1779], facsimile edition (Olney: The Cowper and Newton Museum, 1984), p. viii. (English slightly modernised.)

22 William Cowper, *The Task* (1785), quoted in David Scott, 'Pastoral Tradition in Religious Poetry', p. 733.

23 He is not to be confused with the Scottish minster the Revd Robert Walker, famous as the Skating Minister in Henry Raeburn's painting.

Chapel', in the sonnet sequence *The River Duddon* (1820), Wordsworth goes back once again, and quite deliberately, to Chaucer's Parson and Herbert, recalling:

> those days
> When this low Pile a Gospel Teacher knew,
> Whose good works formed an endless retinue:
> A Pastor such as Chaucer's verse portrays;
> Such as the heaven-taught skill of Herbert drew;
> And tender Goldsmith crowned with deathless praise![24]

Wordsworth is referring, of course to Oliver Goldsmith's saintly Dr Primrose in his novel *The Vicar of Wakefield* (1766). We should not forget that as a young man Wordsworth himself had declared his intention of being ordained, even writing in May 1792 of this being as soon as 'in the approaching winter or spring', and he continued even in his more doubting middle age, in his *Ecclesiastical Sonnets* (1822), to celebrate the history and ceremonies of the Church of England.[25] Earlier in *The Excursion* (1814), Wordsworth describes the pastoral ministry of the clergyman as of one who knows his people, both living and dead, and is a teacher of his flock, yet with humility, pursuing 'forgiveness, patience, hope and charity'.[26]

When, in 1839, Wordsworth was given an honorary degree by Oxford University, the Revd John Keble praised him as a defender of 'high and sacred Truth'. It was Keble's voice which had in effect started the Oxford Movement in 1833 when he preached his Assize Sermon on national apostasy in St Mary's Church, Oxford. The Movement's aim, in brief, was to defend the spiritual and theological independence of the Church of England from the Erastian tendencies of state control through parliament. Keble himself was a prime example of a clergyman that is, sadly, becoming all too rare in our contemporary church as it is overwhelmed by busyness and declining numbers in the ordained ministry. He was a man of immense learning, a fellow and tutor at Oriel College, Oxford and between 1831 and 1841 he was Professor of Poetry at that university. (Keble's *Lectures on Poetry* [1832-41], delivered in Latin, remain some

---

24 William Wordsworth, *Poetical Works*, ed. by Thomas Hutchinson, rev. edn, Ernest de Selincourt (Oxford: Oxford University Press, 1969), p. 300.

25 See, David L. Edwards, *Poets and God* (London: Darton, Longman and Todd, 2005), p. 165.

26 Quoted in David Scott, op. cit. p. 735.

of the finest ever given by a holder of that office.) Yet in 1836 he quietly took the country parish of Hursley in Hampshire and remained serving there for thirty years until his death in 1866. In 1827 Keble had published anonymously a little volume of poems entitled *The Christian Year*. It turned into a persistent best-seller, my own copy, printed in 1909, being bound in black leather with gold tooling and a cross on the front cover – to all intents and purposes appearing like another *Book of Common Prayer*. *The Christian Year* is a collection of poems that follows the church's year through the Anglican *Prayer Book*, together with prayers to accompany the Occasional Offices such as confirmation, matrimony and the funeral service. Its poems are deeply influenced by George Herbert, and some of Keble's verses have also, like Herbert's, survived as hymns: 'New every morning is the love' (for Morning Prayer), 'Blessed are the pure in heart' (for the Purification of Saint Mary the Virgin), and, perhaps less well known now, 'There is a book, who runs may read' (Septuagesima). Keble's poem for the Tuesday in Whitsun-Week is 'addressed to candidates for ordination', and returns us to a familiar theme that we have encountered in Herbert also – that of failure in ministry, or the sense of 'uselessness'. The image in the first stanza is all too familiar.

> "Lord, in Thy field I work all day,
> "I read, I teach, I warn, I pray,
> "And yet these willful wandering sheep
> "Within Thy fold I cannot keep."
>
> . . .
>
> What? wearied out with half a life?
> Scared with this smooth unbloody strife?
> Think where thy coward hopes had flown
> Had Heaven held out the martyr's crown.
>
> How couldst thou hang upon the Cross,
> To whom a weary hour is loss?
> Or how the thorns and scourging brook,
> Who shrinkest from a scornful look?
>
> Yet, ere they craven spirit faints,
> Hear thine own King – the King of saints;
> Though thou wert toiling in the grave,
> 'Tis He can cheer thee, He can save.[27]

27 John Keble, *The Christian Year* [1827] (London: Longmans, Green Co, 1909),

As a poet Keble is no George Herbert, but he is imbued with the same pastoral spirit. The pastoral ministry of the church, he knows very well, is not ours, but is the ministry of Christ in whose service we toil, and in which we are to seek no personal reward or even success. I will return to this constant theme again when we come to consider the pastoral tradition in our own time.

Keble also contributed forty-six poems to a collection of Tractarian verse entitled *Lyra Apostolica* (1836) with poems by other leaders of the Oxford Movement, including, above all, John Henry Newman (who wrote one hundred and nine of the one hundred and seventy-nine poems in the collection), but also Isaac Williams, Hurrell Froude and Robert Isaac Wilberforce. It was Newman, who was at that time vicar of St Mary's, Oxford, who wrote the poem (*Lyra Apostolica* XXXIII) which affirms the centrality of the Eucharist in the Anglicanism of the Oxford Movement, and the importance of faith over understanding:

Whene'er I seek the Holy Altar's rail,
    And kneel to take the grace there offered me,
It is no time to task my reason frail,
    To try Christ's words, and search how they may be;
Enough, I eat His Flesh and drink His Blood,
More is not told – to ask it is not good.[28]

The Christian life is hidden in Christ and is centered upon the sacrament of Holy Communion. This is something that Herbert would have understood perfectly. One of Herbert's successors in translating Psalm 23 for congregational singing was the Revd Sir Henry Williams Baker (1821-77), vicar of Monkland near Leominster from 1851 until his death in 1877 and best known today for his work on the collection known as *Hymns Ancient and Modern* (1861). In Baker's 'translation' the Psalm becomes the familiar hymn 'The king of love my shepherd is', beautifully transformed into a high Anglican celebration of the sacrament with the language of 'unction' and 'chalice':

Thou spread'st a table in my sight;
    Thy unction grace bestoweth;
And oh, what transport of delight
    From thy pure chalice floweth.[29]

---

pp. 117-18.
28 *Lyra Apostolica*. Fourth Edition (Derby: Henry Mozley and Sons, 1840), p. 37.
29 Donald Davie (Ed), *The Psalms in English*, p. 289.

Returning for a moment to John Keble, we realise how his ministry in Hursley is indicative of why no women's voices have, as yet, been heard in this pastoral tradition in English poetry. It is not simply that, until recently, women have been excluded from priestly ordination, though that is an important factor as well. But one of Keble's parishioners was the devout novelist Charlotte Mary Yonge, and it was a rule with him that nothing of her writings were to be published until they had passed the approval of her vicar Mr Keble, who frequently made alterations to the text that she always accepted. Keble warned Miss Yonge, as a woman, against 'too much talk and discussion of church matters, especially doctrines, and against dangers of these things merely for the sake of their beauty and poetry.'[30] Nevertheless, one cannot omit a mention of another devout Tractarian woman writer, Christina Rossetti (1830-94), some of whose poetry has found its way into the pastoral tradition and into English hymnody, above all her beautiful poem 'In the bleak midwinter', its last verse accepting her humble role in our ministry to the infant Jesus – neither a shepherd of a flock, nor a wise man, but a poor woman who can only 'give my heart'. And it was another female poet, the Roman Catholic convert Alice Meynell (1847-1922), who perhaps suggests in her poem 'The Shepherdess' (1895) that the image of the shepherd of the flock is not exclusively male, though she is shepherd only of her own thoughts:

> She walks – the lady of my delight –
>   A shepherdess of the sheep.
> Her flocks are thoughts. She keeps them white;
>   She guards them from the steep;
> She feeds them on the fragrant height,
>   And folds them in for sleep.[31]

Before leaving the nineteenth century there is one priest and poet, another Roman Catholic, who should not be omitted from this very brief review of the English pastoral tradition. Gerard Manley Hopkins (1844-89) was a Jesuit who, following his ordination in 1877, experienced an unhappy and peripatetic pastoral career, unable to reconcile his priestly vocation with his genius as a poet. As a priest he worked in rapid succession in Chesterfield, London, Oxford, then to his

---

30 Quoted in Robert Lee Wolf, *Gains and Losses: Novels of Faith and Doubt in Victorian England* (London: John Murray, 1977), p. 119.

31 Christopher Ricks (Ed), *The New Oxford Book of Victorian Verse* (Oxford: Oxford University Press, 1987), p. 517.

great misery in industrial Liverpool and Glasgow, before returning to teaching, finally at University College, Dublin. He eventually died there of typhoid in June, 1889. His fame as a poet was posthumous, and it was in Dublin that he wrote his six 'terrible sonnets', outbursts of despair about his own life and his relationship with God. They are, perhaps, the most excruciatingly painful poems ever written on the loneliness, the uselessness and the futility of priesthood:

> To seem the stranger lies my lot, my life
> Among strangers. Father and mother dear,
> Brothers and sisters are in Christ not near
> And he my peace/my parting, sword and strife.
>   England, whose honour O all my heart woos, wife
> To my creating thought, would neither hear
> Me, were I pleading, plead nor do I: I wear-
> y of idle a being but by where wars are rife.
>
>   I am in Ireland now; now I am at a third
> Remove. Not but in all removes I can
> Kind love both give and get. Only what word
> Wisest my heart breeds dark heaven's baffling ban
> Bars or hell's spell thwarts. This to hoard unheard,
> Heard unheeded, leaves me a lonely began.[32]

In many ways this poem lies at the very heart of the pastoral tradition in English poetry, though at the same time now far removed from Chaucer's Parson. And yet he, too, was an outsider, though faithful and less despairing than Hopkins, and perhaps simpler. But he also lived in a different age, the age of medieval Christendom, and by the end of the nineteenth century and with accelerated speed in the century to follow, the church was in decline and taken far less seriously, living on the edge of society rather than at its centre. In the twentieth century, the note of 'uselessness' and often despair in the priestly ministry is sounded even more insistently in poetry. The Welsh parish priest and poet R.S. Thomas often expresses the loneliness of the ministry of the priest in the midst of a careless, unbelieving world. His poem 'The Priest', in the words of one contemporary Christian evangelist, Annie R. Eskridge, 'captures well the real nature of our calling and ministry':[33]

---

32 *Poems of Gerard Manley Hopkins*, ed. by Robert Bridges (Oxford: Oxford University Press, 1931), p. 65.
33 Posted on the internet, 5 January, 2012.

The priest picks his way
Through the parish. Eyes watch him
From windows, from the farms;
Hearts wanting him to come near.
The flesh rejects him.[34]

The priest here, the true descendant of Chaucer's Parson, walks through his parish, visiting his flock, and (in a wonderful phrase) 'limping through life/On his prayers'. Thomas, there is no doubt, was a devout man, by and large a reserved and faithful priest, but he is only human and there are times when his temper gets the better of him. In the same collection of poems, *Not That He Brought Flowers* (1968), the poem 'A Priest to his People' opens with a violence, a prejudice even, that takes the breath away:

Men of the hills, wantoners, men of Wales,
With your sheep and your pigs and your ponies, your sweaty females,
How I have hated you for your irreverence, your scorn even
Of the refinements of art and the mysteries of the Church.[35]

The image of the lonely, educated priest isolated among his uneducated, unrefined and uncaring flock is a common one in literature through the centuries. It is part of the cross that must be born, a division denying understanding and articulation as in George Eliot's tragic story of *The Sad Fortunes of the Reverend Amos Barton* in *Scenes of Clerical Life* (1858). But the loneliness that is often at the heart of the pastoral ministry can also have a quiet propriety to it, a being with God in an 'acceptable' way in a world obsessed with success, measurable achievement and efficiency. We return now to David Scott, the Anglican priest and poet with whose essay this chapter began, and find in his poetry a gentle divinity present in the world that is far away from the apparent crass ruthlessness and drive of the current Church of England, if *The Guardian* is to be believed. In his poem 'Early Communion', Scott, with the faithful few in his congregation, returns us to the world of George Herbert and John Keble with an acceptance that over-rides the violence that can erupt in R.S. Thomas, understandable though that is:

34 R.S. Thomas, *Not That He Brought Flowers* (London: Rupert Hart-Davis, 1968), p. 29.

35 Quoted in W. Moelwyn Merchant, *R.S. Thomas* (Fayetteville: The University of Arkansas Press, 1990), p. 8.

Checking times the day before by brushing
blown snow off a leaning board, I guessed
that eight o'clock would chime
on a handful of us, and the priest.
The service was according to the book,
the only variables being
my random fist of coins scooped into a bag
and the winter jasmine above the holy table.
For the rest, we knelt where it advised us to,
Ungainly but meaning it, trusting to the words set
(on paper difficult to separate)
that what we did was acceptable.[36]

As a priest myself, I can enter precisely into this poem, summed up in that final word 'acceptable'. That has to be enough. This is, after all, a 'service' – we do not celebrate early communion for gain or advancement – it is done because the church is a community which serves, and serves God. Scott catches beautifully the tone and atmosphere of the priest and congregation at such a service, 'ungainly, but meaning it'. It is honest, genuine. In his brief poem 'After Mass' Scott again sums up the sense in putting vestments away after a celebration of the sacrament – 'Another day is satisfied'.[37]

Such understatement is a characteristic of the pastoral tradition at its best. Like charity in St Paul's great hymn, such piety 'vaunteth not itself, is not puffed up.' (I Corinthians 13: 4, King James Bible). At its best it has a quiet and unassuming humour (it is there even in Herbert and Cowper if we listen carefully), caught beautifully in David Scott's sequence of poems written as letters in 1932 to Mr Pitt about the church boiler and its woes:

I know you'll understand if I say that a service
held under threat of explosion is not conducive
to the rest and quietness advocated by the Evening Collect.
It makes everyone nervous.[38]

The reference is, of course, to the *Prayer Book* 'Second Collect at Evening Prayer': 'and also that by thee we being defended from the fear of our enemies may pass our time in rest and quietness.' The malfunctioning, probably ancient, church boiler can be an enemy too, sometimes.

---

36 David Scott, *A Quiet Gathering* (Newcastle upon Tyne: Bloodaxe Books, 1984), p. 38.
37 Ibid., p. 39.
38 David Scott, 'The Church Boiler', *Playing for England* (Newcastle upon Tyne: Bloodaxe Books, 1989), p. 47.

But perhaps my favourite poem by David Scott is entitled 'Parish Visit', as it captures precisely the pastoral ministry that we have been tracing since Chaucer's poor Parson. It describes a visit to a home recently bereaved:

> Going about something quite different,
> begging quiet entrance
> with nothing in my bag.[39]

Scott encapsulates in his poem that familiar sense of 'uselessness' – he brings nothing to remedy the situation, but that is precisely why the visit is so important. There is nothing direct, nothing 'efficient' – it just 'is' a communion of souls in which talk is incidental; the conversation is described as 'little runs at understanding'. But, as Newman has taught us – this care is not about understanding, but something else.

And so, finally, we come to a poet that is hardly proper company for the reverend and devout writers with whom we have been journeying in this chapter since Geoffrey Chaucer. Philip Larkin is there because he reminds us that the pastoral tradition is still present even in an age when, it might seem, the church has lost its nerve, or perhaps its relevance for many people, in spite of all its efforts and strivings after business. Society has moved on with, at best for many, just some kind of nostalgia which surfaces at times of baptism or perhaps weddings and funerals. But that is, I think, a little too cynical. Larkin's poem 'Church Going' is included in his early collection entitled *The Less Deceived*, published over sixty years ago. As delicately as David Scott, in his way, the unbeliever Larkin describes his visit to an empty church with its 'tense, musty, unignorable silence', a visit conducted in 'awkward reverence'. (Scott's early morning worshippers, too, were 'ungainly'.) Here is the last verse of 'Church Going':

> A serious house on serious earth it is,
> In whose blent air all our compulsions meet,
> Are recognized, and robed as destinies.
> And that much never can be obsolete,
> Since someone will forever be surprising
> A hunger in himself to be more serious,
> And gravitating with it to this ground,
> Which, he once heard, was proper to grow wise in,
> If only that so many dead lie round.[40]

---

39 Scott, *A Quiet Gathering*, p. 77.
40 Philip Larkin, *The Less Deceived* (Hessle: The Marvell Press, 1955), p. 29.

'He' once heard it from a fellow priest of Chaucer's parson, one supposes. In Larkin's post-Christian poem, the pastoral tradition is still present, its voice typically understated, wise, beyond reason, and serious. In a famous poem in a later collection of verse, 'An Arundel Tomb', Larkin writes of:

> Our almost-instinct almost true:
> What will survive of us is love.[41]

I remember clearly that I was sixteen when I first encountered this poem at school, not so long after I had begun to read Thomas Hardy, Larkin's favourite poet of the previous century, and I have balanced with them ever since on that edge (even as a clergyman) between belief and unbelief that is, I would want to say, where we might be most honest, almost true.

The pastoral tradition in English poetry is, then, very much alive today. Perhaps it is not always in published collections of verse or at the high poetic level of R.S. Thomas or David Scott, but in the many clergy – now, in the Anglican tradition, both men and women – who send me their poems, verses that they find necessary as part of their ministry and their spirituality. The work of the 'Poetry Church' continues, and we have recently had an Archbishop of Canterbury, Rowan Williams, who is also a fine poet. Books continue to be produced and read, like Ruth Etchells' *Praying with the English Poets* (1990) or Malcolm Guite's (himself a fine poet) *Waiting on the Word: A Poem a Day for Advent, Christmas and Epiphany* (2015), keeping poetry at the heart of the church's life and ministry.

What is striking in our age of ecclesial decay and marginalisation is that the 'continuities' of this tradition are as evident and perhaps more important than any changes. David Scott concludes the essay with which I began this chapter with the observation that 'the tradition will inevitably change as the institution changes and will be energised by insights into pastoral care gathered from many different circumstances'.[42] Yet, at the same time, he admits that certain things remain – engagement, compassion, realism, sacrifice and truth. And there are more continuities than these, I think. There is that note of 'uselessness' – which, of course, is not quite that. Rather it is the sense of being in the service of someone or something 'other' than the immediate

---

41 Philip Larkin, *The Whitsun Weddings* (London: Faber and Faber, 1964), p. 46.
42 David Scott, 'Pastoral Tradition in Religious Poetry, p. 740.

demands and ambitions of this world. It is that standing apart, yet at the same time being at the very centre of things that can so easily be neglected by the smart and measurable 'busyness' of the world. It even outstrips belief itself, as we have seen in Philip Larkin, for something always remains. And that something, as in Hardy's poetry, is as hard to eliminate as it is to define, for it lies close to the very heart of a certain identity that is everywhere in English literature. For example, on the first page of George Eliot's first fictional success, *Adam Bede* (1859) we find the eponymous hero, the village carpenter, hard at work while he sings Bishop Thomas Ken's Morning Hymn, 'Awake, my soul, and with the sun . . .'. The Christian hymn is entirely at one with Adam Bede's everyday work – the words lost in moments of particular concentration, then breaking out again:

> Let all thy converse be sincere,
> Thy conscience as the noonday clear. [*sic*]

And with this we are left again with Chaucer's 'povre Persoun of a Toun'. He does not leave or abandon his parish for the advancements of London and St Paul's Cathedral. He tramps out in all weathers in his care for his flock, he 'koude in litel thing have suffisaunce', he is a learned man, such learning being necessary for the true preaching of the gospel, and he is charitable, a 'noble ensample to his sheep'.[43] This Parson is, as a pastor, perhaps few in number but present through the ages and without him the church will be nothing. Nor will he, or she, I suspect, ever entirely disappear. A learned Anglican priest in the twentieth century of poetic disposition though not himself a poet, Dom Gregory Dix, famously encapsulated the sacramental heart of this pastoral tradition, centered upon the Eucharist, writing that 'week by week and month by month, in a hundred thousand successive Sundays, faithfully, unfailingly, across all the parishes of christendom, the pastors have done this [celebrated the Eucharist] just to *make* the *plebs sancta Dei* – the holy common people of God.'[44]

---

43 Geoffrey Chaucer, *The General Prologue*, ll. 477-528.
44 Dom Gregory Dix, *The Shape of the Liturgy* (Westminster: Dacre Press, 1945), p. 744.

8.
Conclusion:
or, Last Words

I began this book on a personal note and I shall end it in the same manner. It should be clear by now, I hope, that the matter of Christianity is something that will not leave me, or perhaps to put it better, from which I have never been able to escape, while the stuff of poetry is at once, for me, the necessary expression and critique that lies at the very heart of that matter. For me the two are inseparable. And so it was that, as soon as I had got over my struggle to say something coherent about Samuel Taylor Coleridge as a poet and a religious thinker in my first book, I tried to do something more general and maybe more ambitious in my second which was entitled *The Study of Literature and Religion* (1989). It must have worked to some degree as it is the only one of my books which has been granted a second edition by its publisher (1992).

I began that book by looking at various collections of English poetry that bear the added word 'religious' (or sometimes 'Christian') in their title. What precisely *is* 'religious (or more particularly 'Christian') poetry'? I append to that list now some collections that have appeared since 1992, and also two collections of Australian poetry, Les Murray's *Anthology of Australian Religious Verse* (1986) and Kevin Hart's *Oxford Book of Australian Religious Verse* (1996).[1] Starting from there and working backwards,

---

1   The list is by no means exhaustive, but rather seeks to be representative. Lord

almost all of these books, with some notable exceptions, begin with an admission of uncertainty as to what this term 'religious poetry', let alone 'Christian poetry', might actually mean at all. In a typically philosophically dense Introduction, Kevin Hart begins his Australian collection with the somewhat unhelpful assertion, 'Needless to say, *religious* is at least as hard to pin down as *poetry*.'[2] Put together the two words become 'religious poetry' and that is even more elusive of clear meaning.

Back in 1940, Lord David Cecil, and in a specifically Christian rather than a more broadly religious setting, seemed less uncertain, but like Dr Samuel Johnson in his *Lives of the Poets* (1779-81), and most particularly in his *Life of Waller*, Cecil expressed a distaste for most religious poetry, the poet generally being not up to the task of coping with an 'emotion [that] is the most sublime known to man' – that is the religious. Cecil writes that:

> Much Christian verse is, by an aesthetic standard, insincere. The writer, that is, does not say what he really feels, but what he thinks he ought to feel: and he speaks not in his own voice but in the solemn tones that seem fitting to his solemn subject.[3]

He is by and large following a slightly earlier and celebrated essay by T.S. Eliot entitled 'Religion and Literature' (1935), in which Eliot writes from the perspective of the reader of poetry:

> For the great majority of people who love poetry, '*religious* poetry' is a variety of *minor* poetry: the religious poet is not a poet who is treating the whole subject matter of poetry in a religious spirit, but a poet who is dealing with a confined part of the subject matter: who is leaving out what men consider is their major passions, and therefore confessing his ignorance of them . . .

David Cecil (Ed), *The Oxford Book of Christian Verse* (Oxford: Clarendon Press, 1940); Donald Davie (Ed), *The New Oxford Book of Christian Verse* (Oxford: Oxford University Press, 1981); Peter Levi, *The Penguin Book of English Christian Verse* (Harmondsworth: Penguin, 1984); Helen Gardner (Ed), *The Faber Book of Religious Verse* (London: Faber and Faber, 1972); Alwyn Marriage (Ed), *New Christian Poetry* (London: Collins, 1990).

2   Kevin Hart, Introduction to *The Oxford Book of Australian Religious Verse* (Oxford: Oxford University Press, 1996), p. xvi.

3   Lord David Cecil, *The Oxford Book of Christian Verse* (Oxford: Clarendon Press, 1940), p. xiii.

But what is more, I am ready to admit that up to a point these critics are right.[4]

I can see, of course, what Lord Cecil and Eliot mean, and to a degree even agree with them. A great deal of religious poetry is indeed at best insipid. But in addition I have long thought that it is not really correct to speak of the 'Christian poet' but rather of the poet who happens to be a Christian. In the end, a poet is a poet, and religion and Christianity can indeed become belittlements of poetry if they intrude too far and in the wrong way. Such is also essentially the position taken up by both Donald Davie and Peter Levi in their introductions to *The New Oxford Book of Christian Verse* and *The Penguin Book of English Christian Verse* respectively. Levi states the obvious with, perhaps, a degree of mock solemnity, that 'poetry itself is not a precisely Christian activity'.[5] Even Alwyn Marriage in her more devotional and contemporary collection entitled *New Christian Poetry* (1990) admits that 'devotional literature, however perceptive and inspiring, is not necessarily great poetry'.[6] Helen Gardner, it seems to me, simply side-steps the issue of the nature of the power and authority of 'poetics' by accepting as her criterion in her collection 'that a religious poem [is] a poem concerned in some way with revelation and with man's response to it'.[7] In a way that is true, but this is one of those statements that is simply too broad to be helpful, a manner of speaking to which, it must be admitted, professors of English Literature are rather prone.

What I have tried to do in this book is something rather different. I am not concerned with compiling an anthology that has to be, in some sense, representative of some tradition or culture. My selection of poets and one particular tradition of pastoral poetry has been purely personal and it is not even historically consecutive. All of my poets, from the deeply devout to the deeply troubled, have had some close connection with the Anglican tradition, or even more particularly the Church of England, and that is, of course, my own tradition. But it is

---

4   T.S. Eliot, *Selected Essays*. Third Edition (London: Faber and Faber, 1951), p. 390.

5   Peter Levi, Introduction to *The Penguin Book of English Christian Verse* (Harmondsworth: Penguin, 1984), p. 19.

6   Alwyn Marriage, Foreword to *New Christian Poetry* (London: Collins, 1990), p. 9. Her collection is closer to the poems of the 'Poetry Church' referred to in the discussion of the pastoral tradition in English verse.

7   Helen Gardner, Preface to *The Faber Book of Religious Verse* (London: Faber and Faber, 1972), p. 7.

the close yet tricky relationship between poetry and Christian belief or unbelief that has held my attention, and all of my poets, I would argue, are in their different ways deeply 'religious'. Furthermore, rather than religious poetry as such I am more fascinated by the nature of religious *language* in poetry, a poetics perhaps – that is the power of the words and diction by which poets seek to articulate their sense of God, or perhaps their lack of it. We have seen that for Samuel Taylor Coleridge the words themselves are living and powerful, resisting reduction to plain meaning and expressive of mysteries that are finally beyond the words themselves. Poets, then, live on the very knife-edge of language (an image to which I will return in a moment), at the point at which meaning tips over into something more vast and elusive, yet shedding a light on human experience and what exactly it is to 'know' something or someone.

In the specific field of liturgy, or Christian worship, this was the subject of my last book, *The Language of Liturgy* (2018), which attempted to establish the foundations of what I called a 'ritual poetics'. I tried to argue that the Anglican devotion to the *Book of Common Prayer* should never be reduced to vague nostalgia for past glories in the church but rather is rooted in a density in the English language as it emerged from the late Middle Ages alongside the Petrarchan poetics of the European Renaissance, and then met the complex theological debates of the English Reformation. People like Archbishop Thomas Cranmer knew very well that a word misplaced could cost you your life – words were powerful and in many ways, for they were also the gateway to the glory of God as well as to the hell of the scaffold (though these could be the same road). The Cranmerian liturgical impulse sought, I suggested in my book, 'a form of words . . . that glorifies the incomprehensibility – the unboundedness – of God in an eschatological vision that stretches, in the very tropes and liveliness of words, between heaven and earth.'[8]

I do not wish here to qualify this statement or diminish its language. It is often noted, and I have said it more than once in this book, that we live today in a very utilitarian age, our sense of language enervated by the shreds of logical positivism and obsessed with the demand that all our aims and objectives, and their outcomes, be measurable and technologically precise. But it remains the case that 'where there is no vision, the people perish'. (Proverbs 29: 18). That remains as true

---

8   David Jasper, *The Language of Liturgy* (London: SCM, 2018), p. 17.

as ever. The church itself, as both Thomas Hardy and S.T. Coleridge deeply felt in their different ways, could sometimes obscure that vision, the church its own worst enemy in the attempted realisation of the sense of the divine in human life. I have come to feel very strongly that the concern for contemporary liturgical reformers for comprehensibility and a language that can be readily understood is a profound and even dangerous mistake. As living, unifying things, words can never be merely a means to an end, for they are, in all their poetic mystery, an end in themselves – and it is the vocation of the poet to speak words that are themselves part of the mystery: language as sacramental, the words of the poet irreplaceable, irreduceable, being what they are. This is where poetry and religion meet – not in definitions or statements but in something far more important. The great English theologian Austin Farrer, one of the most profoundly poetic spirits in the English church in the twentieth century wrote at the end of his Bampton Lectures delivered in Oxford in 1948 and entitled *The Glass of Vision*:

> Poetry and divine inspiration have this in common, that they are both projected in images which cannot be decoded, but must be allowed to signify what they signify of the reality beyond them. In this respect inspiration joins hands with poetry.[9]

Those people who attempt to write the prayers of our liturgy should pay attention to this. Words in poetry – and in the particular poetry of liturgical utterance – are not a means to an end but an end in themselves. They cannot be replaced. It is for this reason that I feel so uncomfortable with some words in the Preface of the *Alternative Service Book* (1980) of the Church of England, words which I suspect my own father may have had a hand in as the then Chairman of the Church of England Liturgical Commission. My criticism, then, is not unkindly meant:

> But words, even agreed words, are only the beginning of worship. Those who use them do well to recognize their transience and imperfection; to treat them as a ladder, not a goal; to acknowledge their power in shaping faith and kindling devotion, without claiming that they are fully adequate to the task. Only [*sic*] the grace of God can make up what is lacking in the faltering words of men.[10]

---

9   Austin Farrer, *The Glass of Vision* (Westminster: Dacre Press, 1948), p. 148.
10 Preface to *The Alternative Service Book* (Cambridge: Cambridge University

I understand the sentiment, but this represents a profound misjudgment about words and language that this whole book has sought to dispel. Words are not simply the beginning of worship.

This book, furthermore, has been about poets and their poetry rather than about critics. As one of this latter breed myself, though in a lowly station, I have always been both haunted and reassured by that exchange of insults in Samuel Beckett's play *Waiting for Godot* between Valdimir and Estragon that descends to single words: Moron! Vermin! Abortion! Sewer-rat! Curate! Cretin! (with finality) Crritic! – from which Vladimir 'wilts, vanquished, and turns away'.[11] But then there are moments when the acute critical mind can enter with genuine imagination into the complexity of the poetic world. I have long been an admirer of A.D. Nuttall's book *Overheard By God: Fiction and Prayer in Herbert, Milton, Dante and St. John* (1980). Nuttall does not claim to be a Christian, but he does bring God into the equation of his literary criticism:

> This study begins with an intuition: that for much of our older literature one may suppose the presence of an extra (and inhuman) reader: that which is written for man is always and necessarily read also by God. The bourgeois marriage of poet and reader which now dominates literature and criticism was once infiltrated by a third party, whose claims are both more importunate and more absolute than those of any ordinary lover.[12]

I love the acidity in that phrase 'the bourgeois marriage of poet and reader'. Beginning with the poetry of George Herbert, Nuttall ends with the poetics of the Fourth Gospel. He concludes with a reading of John 18: 33-38, as an example of what he calls 'discontinuous dialogue', that is the conversation between Jesus and Pontius Pilate that ends with Pilate's famous question about truth. To cut a long argument short, Nuttall, keeping to natural explanations, is convinced that this Jesus is just mad. He can hardly be called wicked, and Nuttall is careful to point out that madness does not, in any sense, preclude considerable intelligence. ('In fact, most dull-witted people are sane and many mad

---

Press, 1980), p. 11

11 Samuel Beckett, *Waiting for Godot* (London: Faber and Faber, 1956), p. 75.

12 A.D. Nuttall, *Overheard By God* (London: Methuen, 1980), p. ix.

people are luminously intelligent'.[13]) But though he suspects that Jesus is deranged and told lies, this is not quite the end of the matter. The Gospel of John, Nuttall suggests, takes its reader to a knife-edge (that phrase again) upon which he or she must balance, whether from a position or belief or unbelief. So he moves to the last words of his book – words of upsetting honesty: 'This barbarous reader took no belief to his reading of the Gospel. But the first thing he encountered was a frontal challenge to that unbelief'.[14]

It is that 'frontal challenge' that has been with me all through the writing of this book, a challenge that resides somehow in the life of words as they bite, caress, console and terrify. In poetry, that which (or the being whom) we call God will not leave us alone, whether we believe in him or her or not. A claim is made upon us.

Since I began my journey with literature and religion so many years ago the world, for me at least, has become a much smaller place. For the last ten years I have been a long distance commuter between Glasgow in Scotland and Beijing in China, teaching in universities in both cities. In my life, too, I have been privileged to reside in India as a schoolteacher, and spent considerable amounts of time teaching in both the United States and Australia. I mention this simply to preface my experience of literature and religion within a much broader context and to offer my sense (it is not a theory) that 'literature' is universal while 'religion', in its particular expressions, is far more culturally specific. Within the constrictions of my lamentable linguistic limitations I have of late participated in the project known as 'Sino-Christian theology' – and increasingly wonder whether Christianity as we know it in the west, its theology built upon the principles of late Greek philosophy, is even possible in China with its very different, far more ancient and Confucian traditions. Religions can be culturally very specific. But, on the other hand, there are ancient Chinese poems and writings that speak immediately and resonate with me at once though I do not profess to 'understand' them in any simple sense, or perhaps in any sense at all. I read the *Tao Te Ching* of Lao Tzu as pure poetry and I respond immediately precisely because I do NOT understand, and I am not meant to. Here is Chapter 25 of the *Dao*:

---

13 Ibid., p. 142.
14 Ibid., p. 143.

There is a thing confusedly formed,
Born before heaven and earth.
Silent and void
It stands alone and does not change,
Goes round and does not weary.
It is capable of being the mother of the world.
I know not its name
So I style it 'the way'.
I give it the makeshift name of 'the great'.
Being great, it is further described as receding,
Receding, it is described as far away,
Being far away, it is described as turning back.[15]

Even in this western, English translation I feel with the rhythm and swing of this pure poetry, its oppositions and necessary contraries. Coleridge would have felt and heard them far more – which is different from saying that one exactly *understands* anything.

Poetry can find us in strange places. Some years ago I attended a Sunday morning Eucharist with a Chinese colleague in St John's Cathedral, Hong Kong. It was a blistering summer day and there were only fans, no air-conditioning, in the cathedral. Yet the choir and priests were in full Anglican liturgical robes and vestments, worn without compromise. The sermon was preached by an elderly English priest who, I later learnt, had been serving in Hong Kong for many years. In a light cotton shirt and trousers I was bathed in sweat. He, on the other hand, wore a cassock, a cassock alb and a heavy chasuble: and he preached for nearly half an hour. It was a wonderful sermon, interwoven with lines from George Herbert and John Donne, and taking us (or perhaps just me) back to New College in Oxford where he had been a student forty years before. I say 'me' because more or less everyone else in the congregation, it seemed, was Asian or local. Few, if any, will have even been to Oxford, I suspect – and I wondered what they could possibly make of this most English of sermons preached in the sub-tropical heat of Hong Kong. But I sensed also a profound atmosphere of the mystery of holiness – what Tony Nuttall would have called a frontal attack on unbelief. It was there in the poetry that was at once ludicrously out of place and yet perfectly at home – a moment of both conformity and rebellion.

---

15 *Tao Te Ching*, trans. by D.C. Lau (Harmondsworth: Penguin, 1963), p. 27.

We often reflect now on the future of the Christian Church in our western culture. Some Christian communities, of course, are thriving, though the older churches are generally disintegrating and collapsing inwards on themselves. This is not the place to analyse their futures, but of one thing I am convinced. Just as Chaucer's Parson of a Town will never quite disappear, neither will the poetry of which I have been writing. Our technological societies have inflicted cruel wounds upon the languages that we speak, but the living mystery of words will never quite be eradicated. Poets will continue to write and speak in words that express belief and unbelief with a seriousness that can never be quite sniggered away. Perhaps it is because poets speak in the language of the imagination, a repetition in the finite mind of the eternal act of creation in the infinite I AM. They speak words as close as human being can reach to the language of God, a continual reminder that in the beginning was the Word, and the Word was with God, and the Word was God. (John 1: 1). God speaks to Job the man of faith in words of power and 'of things too wonderful for me, which I knew not' (Job 42: 3), or he speaks with a still, small voice of the most intense silence (I Kings 19: 12). Perhaps, in the end the poets are so important, and will continue to be so, because they are ones who do not so much speak, but truly listen. In the words of R.S. Thomas:

> Prompt me, God;
> But not yet. When I speak
> Though it be you who speak
> Through me, something is lost.
> The meaning is in the waiting.[16]

---

16 R.S. Thomas, 'Kneeling', in *Not That He Brought Flowers* (London: Rupert Hart-Davis, 1969), p. 32.

Reading List

This reading list is intended to be no more than a brief and selective guide, and assumes that the poems of Thomas Hardy and Samuel Taylor Coleridge are easily available in collected editions and volumes of selected poems.

Thomas Traherne, because his writings almost disappeared and have only recently re-emerged, as I have described, is perhaps less accessible. The vast and excellent *Collected Works* in nine volumes, edited by Jan Ross, some still as yet unpublished by Boydell and Brewer, are expensive and they are research items. Most of the references in my chapter are to the beautifully selected writings, edited by Denis Inge.

Thomas Traherne: *Poetry and Prose* (London: SPCK, 2002).

Sir Philip Sidney's writings in prose and verse are also widely available in a number of editions and selections, but the fairly recent Oxford World Classics edition of *The Sidney Psalter* is excellent and inexpensive.

Hannibal Hamlin, Michael G. Brennan, Margaret P. Hannay and Noel J. Kinnamon, (Eds) *The Sidney Psalter: The Psalms of Sir Philip and Mary Sidney* (Oxford: Oxford University Press, 2009).

The collected poems of Sir Geoffrey Hill have recently become available in one volume which contains all of the poems discussed in this book.

Sir Geoffrey Hill, *Broken Hierarchies: Poems 1952-2012*, ed. by Kenneth Haynes (Oxford: Oxford University Press, 2013).

There are no collections of poetry in the pastoral tradition as I have discussed it here. But a few books have extended discussions that are useful, including the essay by David Scott.

Andrew W. Hass, David Jasper and Elisabeth Jay, (Eds), *The Oxford Handbook of English Literature and Theology* (Oxford: Oxford University Press, 2007).

J.A.W. Bennett, *Poetry of the Passion: Studies in Twelve Centuries of English Verse* (Oxford: Clarendon Press, 1982).

David L. Edwards, *Poets and God: Chaucer, Shakespeare, Herbert, Milton, Wordsworth, Coleridge, Blake* (London: Darton, Longman and Todd, 2005).

Mark Knight, (Ed), *The Routledge Companion to Literature and Religion* (London: Routledge, 2016).

There are many collections of religious or Christian verse in English. The following is a small selection that I have found most valuable, some now quite old, but age, as far as I am aware, is not a crime:

Robert Atwan and Laurance Wieder, (Eds), *Chapters into Verse: Poetry in English Inspired by the Bible*. 2 Volumes. (Oxford: Oxford University Press, 1993).

Lord David Cecil, (Ed.) *The Oxford Book of Christian Verse* (Oxford: Clarendon Press, 1940).

Donald Davie, Ed. *The New Oxford Book of Christian Verse* (Oxford: Oxford University Press, 1981).

Donald Davie, (Ed.), *The Psalms in English* (Harmondsworth: Penguin, 1996).

Colin Duriez, (Ed.), *The Poetic Bible* (London: SPCK, 2001)

Helen Gardner, (Ed.), *The Faber Book of Religious Verse* (London: Faber and Faber, 1972).

Peter Levi, (Ed.), *The Penguin Book of English Christian Verse* (Harmondsworth: Penguin, 1984).

Alwyn Marriage, (Ed.), *New Christian Poetry* (London: Collins, 1990).

Finally, there are countless books, usually of a very modest size, that offer a selection of poems as a help to prayer or following the liturgical year. I have these two helpful suggestions:

Ruth Etchells, *Praying with the English Poets* (London: SPCK, 1990).

Malcolm Guite, *Waiting on the Word: A Poem a Day for Advent, Christmas and Epiphany* (Norwich: Canterbury Press, 2015).

The Poetry Church: An Inclusive Congregation, was founded by an Anglican priest, the late John Waddington-Feather. It continues to be published as a magazine twice a year with a *Poetry Church Collection* published each spring under the editorship of Tony Reavill by Moorside Words and Music. In its description it states that 'the magazine has a pastoral role as well as a literary one'.

Index

#0026 - 051118 - C0 - 234/156/8 - PB - 9780718895419